# Praise for *Embracing Shame*

"A few times in a lifetime a book comes along that opens up the dark recesses of our lives and illuminates the mysteries of human behavior, including why people act the way they do and why there is so much emotional suffering in the world. *Embracing Shame* by Bret Lyon and Sheila Rubin is such a book. It is engaging, transformative, and eye opening! Shame is itself shameful, and so it doesn't get talked about, instead lurking in the shadows, interfering with our ability to give and receive true connection. So it's already a huge contribution to write, as Lyon and Rubin do, in a non-shaming way about shame. But there's more: chapter by chapter, with personal stories and supportive healing exercises, this book builds up a picture of where shame comes from, what it can do, and how it can be transformed. *Embracing Shame* is personal, practical, wise, and ultimately hopeful. I truly wish the whole world would read it, because I want to live in what would then be a safer and more connected world."

ANN WEISER CORNELL, PHD
CEO of Focusing Resources and author of *The Radical Acceptance of Everything*

"Heartwarming, empowering, vulnerable, and brilliant. Every so often, a book comes along that will inspire your mind, touch your soul, and remind you that you are not alone. *Embracing Shame* by Sheila Rubin and Bret Lyon is a groundbreaking book that can help you break free of the chains of shame. Through stories, concrete practices, and research, Sheila and Bret bring us face-to-face with shame's power to paralyze our lives while also offering a way out through embracing it. Steeped in a deep understanding of the body–mind connection, this remarkable guide offers essential strategies for connecting with oneself and with others—and creating a new way forward, one in which shame doesn't define who you are. If shame has been holding you back, *Embracing Shame* can help you let go of those chains and live your life fully. Through powerful stories of recovery and personal growth, the authors show you that it's possible to move beyond shame and create a new path for yourself, your clients, and those you love."

ALBERT WONG, PHD
director of the Trauma Certificate Program at Somatopia

"Bret Lyon and Sheila Rubin have already transformed the trauma therapy field with their Healing Shame workshops. Now anybody who picks up this book can benefit from their rdical healing approach to shame. They have written a gem of a book that anybody can read, understand, relate to, and apply to themselves, to clients, to loved ones. Expect to learn, expect to have 'aha' moments, expect to be moved, expect to be transformed. Not only do Bret and Sheila explain and teach with clarity what shame is, how it affects body and psyche, and what to do when it overtakes us, but with skill, compassion, and bravery they model for us the transforming power of vulnerability and transparency. Leading by example, they show us how to embrace shame by sharing not only examples from their own therapy and coaching practices but also their own experiences of both shame and its healing. I love this book and am grateful that it now exists. Get this book, and your nervous system, as well as your friends and family, will thank you for so doing. Kudos to Bret and Sheila for a spectacular and accessible achievement."

DIANA FOSHA, PHD
developer of AEDP, editor of *Undoing Aloneness and the Transformation of Suffering into Flourishing*, and author of *The Transforming Power of Affect*

"*Embracing Shame* is the clearest, most brilliant, user-friendly book that I've seen on this powerful and misunderstood emotion. Bret and Sheila are among the world's leading experts on shame. They shed a bright light on this elusive emotion and the sneaky ways it shows up in our lives and suppresses our life energy and joy. Through striking examples and carefully crafted exercises, this easy-to-read book will help you understand the toxic effects of shame—guiding you to turn gently toward it rather than experience it as a dreaded enemy, empowering you to learn, grow, and transform your life. I highly recommend this book if you want to recognize and heal the shame that may be holding you back in your life, which can free you up to live a richer life and deepen your relationships."

JOHN AMODEO, PHD
author of *Dancing with Fire* and *Psychology Today* contributor

"This book is an exquisite work on shame. It is revolutionary, insightful, and brilliant. *Embracing Shame* has the capacity to inspire individual and cultural transformation. Sheila and Bret beautifully incorporate both social and psychological aspects of shame, which is essential for any real understanding of shame. Their superb illustration of emotional binds illuminates the importance of how shame binds with other emotions—anger, grief, fear, joy—in everyday life, trapping us in old patterns. Working with shame is multidimensional work, they say. When we recognize where we have broken interpersonal bridges, work to repair them, and accept our imperfections and limitations, then we can finally begin to transform our shame. Though it is written in a way that can benefit anyone, no professional should be without a copy of this book."

SUZANNE RETZINGER, PHD, MFT
coauthor of *Emotions and Violence*

"*Embracing Shame* is a remarkably insightful and thorough guide to the inner experience and complex inner workings of shame. It is wise and compassionate counsel from two superb teachers, communicated with warmth and humanity, and will be of enormous help to anyone who struggles under the oppressive power of this life-choking emotion."

BRUCE ECKER, LMFT
codirector of the Coherence Psychology Institute, co-originator
of Coherence Therapy, and coauthor of *Unlocking the Emotional Brain*

"Bret Lyon and Sheila Rubin have created a much-needed resource. Shame is something we all need to learn much more about, as it is an insidious emotion that has great power to harm us if we are not aware of shame in our daily lives and interactions. This book can truly help us understand and soften shame so it causes far less harm—and can even be helpful. As a trauma psychotherapist and emotions educator, I'm thrilled to have a powerful new book that focuses on healing and transforming shame to recommend to my clients."

HILARY JACOBS HENDEL, LCSW
author of *It's Not Always Depression* and
mental health consultant for AMC's *Mad Men*

"*Embracing Shame* is not only a gem of a book, it makes an extraordinarily important contribution to an area of psychology that is largely overlooked. With powerful examples and mindful exercises, Bret and Sheila show how easy it is to rebalance your nervous system and transform shame in a way that will revitalize your life."

MARK ROBERT WALDMAN
faculty at Holmes Institute, neuroscience researcher,
and coauthor of *How God Changes Your Brain*

"Sheila Rubin and Bret Lyon have long focused their psychotherapeutic and educational work on healing shame. Now readers can access their experience, teachings, and wisdom through their book, which offers hopeful, down-to-earth, and compassionate reflections, as well as guidance, on transforming shame. *Embracing Shame* is a practical and inspiring book not only for clinicians but for everyone who experiences shame— meaning everyone!"

RENÉE EMUNAH, PHD
author of *Acting for Real*, co-editor of *Current Approaches
in Drama Therapy* and *The Self in Performance*, and founder/director of the
Drama Therapy Program at the California Institute of Integral Studies

"*Embracing Shame* shines a spotlight on the most deeply disturbing of all human emotions. Here we see shame's impact on identity, its role in shaping self-esteem, and how it becomes an impediment to intimacy. Bret Lyon and Sheila Rubin illustrate the power of shame to capture and cripple us and reveal the hidden power released by healing shame."

GERSHEN KAUFMAN, PHD
author of *Shame: The Power of Caring* and *The Psychology of Shame*,
coauthor of *Coming Out of Shame*

"Bret and Sheila are pioneers in the work of healing shame, and this book is an essential text. They lay out a clear therapeutic pathway that integrates the latest science of the brain and nervous system, as well as clinical skills. I've learned so much from them that informs my own work."

RUTH L. SCHWARTZ, PHD
director of Conscious Girlfriend Academy and
coauthor of *Conscious Lesbian Dating and Love*

"As a psychiatrist and psychotherapist, I have seen many people whose everyday lives are greatly limited by their shame. I am thrilled that I can now recommend that they read this book. It gives them the theoretical concepts and the practical tools to help them to both understand and transform their shame. It is filled with powerfully moving stories of case examples and demonstrations, as well as exercises you can do on your own or with a trusted partner. After reading and practicing some of the exercises in this book, you may find yourself much more able to get mad and to laugh and to cry and to love."

BARBARA MCCOARD, MD
coauthor of *Sandplay*

"*Embracing Shame* is a wonderful book! I'm delighted to see Bret and Sheila's powerful, transformative, and deeply humane approach to healing shame presented in this engaging format. I love its organization, layout, and accessibility, and I'm eager to share it with colleagues and clients."

FRAN SCHWARTZ, PHD, LCSW
anthropologist and psychotherapist

"I was brought to tears reading through this book. I am so delighted and moved that this now exists in the world. Only through starting to heal my own lifelong shame with the help of Bret, Sheila, and the Healing Shame community have I been able to accept, sit with, and guide my clients through transforming their own. This is life-changing work, a book that is easy to follow and grasp yet has the potential to shift the way you see yourself and the world around you. I believe it contains the power of an earthquake— shifting the tectonic plates of our culture and mindset about shame."

LAUREN GRAY, LMFT
Healing Shame Practitioner

"As a longtime student of the profound work on healing shame that Bret Lyon and Sheila Rubin have created, I am beyond excited that they have been able to bring so many of their concepts and stories into this book. They teach that healing shame is very possible when we stop fearing it and embrace its purpose for us. In my years of working with shame, I have felt the loosening effect of recognizing it for what it is, how it shows itself, and why. This more compassionate way of seeing shame as an overprotective part that needs tactful attention has brought transformation within myself, in my marriage, and to the educators and students I have worked with over the years."

ELIZABETH DAVIDGE
Center for Healing Shame workshop coordinator and
founder of re-SOURCING Resiliency for educators and youth

"With clarity and compassion, Bret and Sheila have provided a Rosetta Stone–like guide to understanding, unearthing, and healing this painful, mysterious, and often invisible emotion. The effects of shame are pervasive throughout medicine and the health-care world—the healing profession is in dire need of healing."

HARALD BETTGER, MD
educator on shame in medicine

"Sheila Rubin and Bret Lyon have written a masterful, transformational, comprehensive, and user-friendly guide to understanding and working with shame. It is written in a style that feels as if the authors were having a relaxed conversation with you. The easy-to-follow explanations and creative experiential exercises will help you 'embrace shame' by transforming toxic shame into healthy shame. This book is especially important for parents in raising secure, confident children and for couples wanting a more loving relationship. Reading this reconnected me with how to work more creatively with my own shame and that of my clients. I would call this book 'the ultimate guide to healing shame.'"

JAN DISANTO, RN, MFT
Gottman and EFT couples therapist and author of *Myrtle the Turtle Discovers Hug Power*

"If you're human, you must read this book! All that you need to understand shame is within these pages. The tools and exercises can and should be used by everyone. If you're raising a child who has been separated from their family of origin, Bret and Sheila have provided the tools you need to heal the pain that these childhood wounds create. What a world we could create if we could all turn shame into valuable medicine. Bravo!"

JULINE AGUILAR
director of the Foster and Kinship Care Education Program at Folsom Lake College

# Embracing Shame

### Also by Bret Lyon and Sheila Rubin

*Healing Shame: How to Work with This Powerful, Mysterious Emotion—And Transform It into an Ally*, 6-CD audio program, Sounds True, 2021.

"Healing Shame and Developing Healthy Shame in the Imaginal Realm" in *Action Explorations: Using Psychodramatic Methods in Non-Therapeutic Settings*, Adam Blatner, editor, 2019.

### Also by Bret Lyon

*The Bret Lyon Personal Power Program*, Medallion Books, 1986.

### Also by Sheila Rubin

"Shame Clues: From Embarrassment to Breakthrough"—presentation for TEDxSanRafaelWomen, November 2020.

"Unpacking Shame and Healthy Shame: Therapy on the Phone or Internet" in *Combining the Creative Therapies with Technology: Using Social Media and Online Counseling to Treat Clients*, Stephanie L. Brooke, editor, 2017.

"Embodied Life Stories: Transforming Shame Through Self-Revelatory Performance" in *The Self in Performance*, Susana Pendzik, Renée Emunah, David Read Johnson, editors, 2016.

"Almost Magic: Working with the Shame That Underlies Depression; Using Drama Therapy in the Imaginal Realm" in *The Use of the Creative Therapies in Treating Depression*, Stephanie L. Brooke and Charles E. Myers, editors, 2016.

"Shame and Countertransference" in *CAMFT – The Therapist magazine*, November/December 2016.

"Myth, Mask and Movement: Ritual Theater in a Community Setting" in *Ritual Theatre: The Power of Dramatic Ritual in Personal Development Groups and Clinical Practice*, Claire Schrader, editor, 2011.

"Women, Food and Feelings: Drama Therapy with Women Who Have Eating Disorders" in *The Creative Therapies and Eating Disorders*, Stephanie L. Brooke, editor, 2007.

"Self-Revelatory Performance" in *Interactive and Improvisational Drama: Varieties of Applied Theatre and Performance*, Adam Blatner, MD, editor, 2007.

# Embracing Shame

How to Stop Resisting Shame
& Turn It into a Powerful Ally

BRET LYON, PHD &
SHEILA RUBIN, MA, LMFT

sounds true
BOULDER, COLORADO

Sounds True
Boulder, CO

This book is not intended as a substitute for the medical recommendations of physicians, mental health professionals, or other health-care providers. Rather, it is intended to offer information to help the reader cooperate with physicians, mental health professionals, and health-care providers in a mutual quest for optimal well-being. We advise readers to carefully review and understand the ideas presented and to seek the advice of a qualified professional before attempting to use them.

All names used throughout the book have been changed to protect student and client privacy.

Published 2023

Cover design by Lisa Kerans
Book design by Ranee Kahler

Printed in the United States of America

BK06610

Library of Congress Cataloging-in-Publication Data

Names: Lyon, Bret, author. | Rubin, Sheila, author.
Title: Embracing shame : how to stop resisting shame and turn it into a
powerful ally / Bret Lyon, PhD, and Sheila Rubin, MA, LMFT.
Description: Boulder, CO : Sounds True, 2023. | Includes bibliographical references.
Identifiers: LCCN 2023005677 (print) | LCCN 2023005678 (ebook) |
    ISBN 9781649630469 (paperback) | ISBN 9781649630476 (ebook)
Subjects: LCSH: Shame. | Self-help techniques.
Classification: LCC BF575.S45 L96 2023 (print) | LCC BF575.S45 (ebook) |
    DDC 152.4--dc23/eng/20230615
LC record available at https://lccn.loc.gov/2023005677
LC ebook record available at https://lccn.loc.gov/2023005678

To our students, clients, friends, and families,
without whom this book would not be possible.


And in memoriam to Bret's Aunt Daisy,
who was a calm anchor for Bret growing up
and "best man" at our wedding,
and Sheila's high school best friend, Patty Rogover Owens,
who saw the inner beauty under Sheila's shyness.
Their reaching out with kindness was lifesaving.
They shined light in the darkness.


And to Tigger II—constant companion,
friend to all, spiritual teacher.

# CONTENTS

CONTENTS

# INTRODUCTION

We wrote this book to bring awareness to something that far too often stays hidden. If you judge yourself harshly; if you've ever frozen up or felt suddenly embarrassed, anxious, or confused without understanding why; if you work hard to do everything right so no one will suspect there's something's wrong with you; or if something from your past often troubles you and sneaks into your thoughts when it's not wanted, this book is for you. Like countless others, you may be affected by one of the most powerful, painful, and invisible emotions: shame. And if you're ready to free yourself from the debilitating beliefs and habits that shame can cause, we invite you to join us on this healing journey.

We're a husband-and-wife team who founded the Center for Healing Shame. We've taught our Healing Shame workshops to thousands of therapists, clinicians, teachers, coaches, nurses, and helping professionals worldwide for almost two decades. We are proud to call these helping professionals our students. Along the way, we've fostered a network of Healing Shame professionals dedicated to helping people internationally. We're on a mission to educate as many people as possible on how to heal shame.

Most people feel they never received proper operating directions for their life. In this book, you'll learn some of those missing instructions, and you'll learn to not judge yourself—whether stepping on the scale, putting on a swimsuit, working on that writing project, or even making love. You'll learn to not criticize yourself for reading one book instead of two, for saying the wrong thing to your kids, or for messing up an assignment at work. You'll experience more balance and have an inner support coach available at all times. You'll learn to integrate all the pieces of yourself to become more authentic and express what you're feeling. You'll learn more ways to replenish yourself, remain grounded, and move forward in life in the way you truly want.

A major part of being human involves being a social creature who needs others. We need others to understand us, and it can feel debilitating when they don't. As a result, we might ruminate afterward, asking ourselves, *What's wrong with me?* or *Was that my fault?* hundreds of times. Far too often, when we share those doubts with others—for example, a close friend or therapist—they encourage us to move on and stop worrying, but then we receive their "helpful" dismissal as more shaming, which only adds to our pain and confusion.

This book is the result of our work with ourselves and with our students and clients. Throughout it, we'll be sharing lots of personal stories, both our own and those of our students, who are all helping professionals, and our clients. All of the stories are true and told with permission. Some are composites, and some details have been changed to assure privacy. In our workshops and private sessions, we try to create a counter-shaming environment—that is, one in which we help lessen the shame people bring in with them—and we hope you experience the same counter-shaming support as you read this book.

Shame is an important and difficult emotion that's far too commonly dismissed and misunderstood. Shame does not simply have to be tolerated. We don't have to remain afraid or ashamed of our shame. Rather than push shame away, strange as this may sound, we encourage our clients and students to embrace it—to acknowledge it, to explore it, and to learn the lessons it is trying to teach. Once we embrace shame, it loses much of its power over us.

There is an old adage that says, "Keep your friends close and your enemies closer." This refers to the idea that we want to know what our enemies are up to so we can be prepared and suffer as little harm as possible. Shame, in its full power, may be an enemy. But shame, when it is understood and softened, can become a friend.

We believe there is an evolutionary purpose to shame, that all societies can benefit from a healthy relationship to shame, and that, if we embrace shame, it can be transformed from a horrifying inner demon to a powerful ally. We believe—as radical as this may sound—that shame can be transformed from toxic and destructive to useful and healthy.

Shame is a difficult and loaded topic, which is why most people avoid talking or thinking about it. As you read this book, we urge you to be gentle with yourself. Go through this material in whatever way feels right to you. You can start at the beginning or go directly to the chapters that pique your interest. You can stop and take a break at any time. We urge you to try some of the practices—they'll offer a more visceral experience that will help all the information this book contains sink in deeper. Above all, be kind to yourself. Make sure you breathe as you read. Put your hand on your heart and remember that you are good enough. If something in the content triggers you, take a break and return to the material whenever it feels right for you.

While this book is written for everyone, much of it can be extremely useful for helping professionals. Most people have trouble coping with shame, and most professionals have trouble helping clients when they are in shame. Additionally, when clients experience shame and react to it, helping professionals will often have their own shame triggered. For that reason, this book contains many tools you can use personally—not only to help you understand and heal your own shame, but also to demystify and heal shame in people you are working with.

1

# Shame—The Magic Emotion

*Shame is a complex and typically hidden emotion. We all experience it. But oftentimes we're not aware of the secret ways it operates.*

—John Amodeo

We want to invite you to welcome all of your emotions as you begin this book. Dealing with shame can be a bumpy ride. Shame can arise at any time, often when you least expect it. As you read, you might experience uncomfortable feelings and realizations, or you might find yourself remembering times in your life that were upsetting and scary. Shame can be a scary and difficult emotion because we are socialized to fear it and therefore avoid it. It takes courage and curiosity to face shame and work with it, but the rewards of doing so can be tremendous.

There's a quality of magic in how powerful and mysterious shame is. We also call shame *the magic emotion* because Sheila was a magician (still is in her own way), and magicians work with misdirection—they distract your attention so you won't see them move the card from their sleeve to their hand or take the coin from behind their back to your ear. All the while, you're convinced you know what's going on.

Shame distracts you by making everything confusing and blurry. Shame focuses you on yourself; it's an incredibly self-conscious emotion. You start focusing more on yourself and less on the people and events around you, getting lost in internal conversations about what's wrong with you, just like a magician's sleight of hand. That's how you lose touch with present reality.

Because shame is so subtle and so powerful, we approach it gently, step-by-step. Shame is a lot like nitroglycerin—a little bit goes a long way. If you don't treat it with respect and care, you might wind up with an explosion. But nitroglycerin in the proper dose can be beneficial—to relax blood vessels and help the heart function properly, for example. That's how shame functions too. Used in the right way, shame is valuable medicine.

## WHAT IS SHAME?

Shame is the opposite of life force, the opposite of what moves us forward, the opposite of what gives us energy and vitality. Shame keeps us stuck; it freezes us. One definition of shame we like to use is this: *shame is both a primary emotion and a state of freeze.* By *primary emotion*, we mean that shame seems to be experienced by people all over the world. Although some animals appear to feel shame, only in humans does shame express itself with exceptional power. By *state of freeze*, we're referring to the unique way that shame disrupts our ability to think clearly. Our attention turns inward, and we become so absorbed in criticizing ourselves that we lose contact with the world.

Brené Brown offers a three-part definition of shame: "the intensely painful feeling or experience of believing that we are flawed and therefore unworthy of love and belonging."[1] Brown's definition describes, first, the physical component of shame—how excruciatingly painful it can be; second, the mental component—the belief that there is something wrong with us; third, we come to believe that, because of our perceived flaws, we are undeserving of love and belonging.

Gershen Kaufman defines shame as "the breaking of the interpersonal bridge."[2] We humans feel safe when we're connected to others. Consciously and unconsciously, we're always on the lookout for connection, and we react strongly when we perceive even the smallest break in attachment, whether between romantic partners, children and their parents or guardians, or friends. The more important the relationship is to us, the greater our emotional wounding when there's a break in attunement. Sometimes what damages the interpersonal bridge might seem minor; it could be as simple as someone looking at their cellphone while you're talking with them. You might try to reason your way out of feeling hurt, but there's something about their behavior that triggers your childhood experience of being ignored and abandoned.

In our work, we often talk about the *90/10 Split*. As a rule, when something relatively small kicks off a powerful shame reaction, 90 percent of that is due to past experiences; only 10 percent is coming from the trigger itself. That's not always the case, of course, but it's almost always true that strong shame experiences have to do with things we had to live through as children.

No matter what causes a rift in the interpersonal bridge, it's crucial to restore the connection. If that doesn't occur, we can be left with toxic shame. The basic formula that applies here is the three Rs: *Relationship, Rupture, Repair.* If there's a rupture and it can be repaired by somebody apologizing or promising to behave differently next time—or there is a compassionate clarifying of what happened—then the shame is minimized and, in fact, can result in what we call *healthy shame.*

Hopefully, these three definitions give you a good sense of how pervasive and important shame is. We believe they also point the way to how we can heal and transform shame. If we view shame as the breaking of the interpersonal bridge, the path to healing begins with rebuilding connection.

**Shame happens in the body as well as the mind.**

## THE PHYSIOLOGY OF SHAME

Shame happens in the body as well as the mind. Shame affects the way we stand, move, breathe, and feel. Our nervous system reads and reacts to a perceived threat, which readies our body to react. The most extreme threat for us humans is exile from our community or family, which often gets triggered when we sense disapproval or humiliation or have the experience of being dismissed or ignored.

When we feel shame, our body starts to contract. Our chest collapses and our head comes forward and lowers so that we are looking down toward our feet rather than out at the world. When the chest collapses like this, it becomes difficult to breathe.

An *action tendency* is a behavior or reaction linked to a particular emotion. The action tendency of shame is to hide, disappear, or freeze in place. Shame makes us feel small, so we shrink physically and mentally. Without being able to breathe fully, our focus narrows. Sometimes it can even be hard to speak or think. Shame severs our access to language and higher-level cognition.

## THE SHAME-PRIDE CONTINUUM

The opposite of shame is pride. Healthy pride is a positive regard for yourself even when you acknowledge limitations and fallibilities. Healthy pride doesn't mean that you think you're better than others; it's the result of accomplishing meaningful goals that have required effort on a foundation of simple positive regard.

On one end of the shame-pride continuum is pride in the self at its best—pride for worthy accomplishments, for example. On the other side of this continuum is the self at its worst—all the stuff we don't want anybody to know or see. At any moment, we're balancing how we show up with ourselves with how we show up with other people, and all of us are performing this balancing act on a regular basis.

It's important to be able to connect with a sense of accomplishment, a sense of achievement. Some people find it hard to contact that experience, but most of us have something in our lives that we're proud of—our children, for example, or maybe somebody we've helped along the way. Most of us also have people in our lives who've helped or inspired us in some way, and it can also ease our feelings of shame to bring them to mind. Our nervous system can start to feel safe again, and the state of freeze we experience in relation to shame can relax.

## PRACTICE

Try to remember something you're proud of. Something you did or said that felt really good. It could be something recent or something that happened a long time ago. Take a deep breath, recall the experience as clearly as you can, and see if you're able to connect with that sense of pride.

## PENDULATING, RESOURCING, AND COUNTER-SHAMING

We want to introduce three concepts to help you stay grounded and present as we go deeper into the material in this book. The first is *pendulating*. Just like the pendulum of a clock, our nervous system never stays put—it moves from one side of the spectrum to the other, calm one minute and excited the next. We can feel quite upset about something and then we cheer up and then eventually we feel gloomy again and so on. It's what our minds naturally do. But shame stops pendulation. When you're frozen in shame—focused on how bad you are and everything that's wrong with you—that's where you'll tend to stay.

## PRACTICE

As you read this book, you may notice shame coming up. That's a natural response. As you read on, we encourage you to feel how much is okay for your nervous system at any given time. If it stops feeling okay, pendulate to thinking about (or doing) something that feels nurturing for you: if it's available to you, get up and move around, look at a favorite picture or painting, talk to a friend, or pet your dog or cat. By taking a break, you can pendulate away from being absorbed in shame and then pendulate back to experiencing it when you feel more ready.

The second concept is *resourcing*. Shame is an under-resourced state that affects the nervous system. When we're in shame, we're basically frozen. It's a protective response in which the amygdala takes over and we lose access to higher-level thinking. You've probably noticed this phenomenon before when arguing with someone who was really activated or when you were the person in the argument who was agitated or triggered.

When we're in shame, we forget we have resources: all the things we do that bring calm and a feeling of competence that tell our nervous system it can relax again. It's crucial that we find and remember resources when working with shame to not get lost in it and cause yet more shame in the process. Resources can be internal or external. Breathing, sensing our feet on the ground, and feeling the energy of our body can be internal resources. External resources include supportive friends, people or pets who've loved us in the past, positive characters in literature or movies, and soothing places we've been to that made us happy or where we felt at peace. Getting in touch with our resources sends signals to the brain and heart that we're safe, and this counters our stress reactions to shame. Our body's state of arousal is quieted, which allows our more evolved systems (rational thought, language, and the ability to see the bigger picture) to come back online.

*Counter-shaming*, the third concept, is more specific to the content of the shame itself. It involves examining the bigger picture and all the details that get lost in the shame freeze, as well as actively countering harmful messages with self-talk.

## PRACTICE

While reading this book, if something triggers a shame reaction and your inner critic starts telling you how deficient you are, be on the lookout for *always* and *never* statements. For example, if you hear your inner voice say something like, *You* never *do it right!* try out a counter-shaming statement such as, *Actually, I got it right yesterday when I . . .* You can counter, *You* always *do that stupid thing they're talking about in this book*, with something like, *Well, maybe I do sometimes, but I often realize it and then change my behavior.* While the inner critic tends to speak in generalities, you can get specific and counter that voice with a more compassionate and realistic look at the situation.

## THE PURPOSE OF SHAME

Every emotion we experience has developed and been refined over thousands (and likely millions) of years of evolution. In proper balance, any emotion is useful. The problem arises when one becomes too powerful and disturbs the balance: we end up with too much of one emotion and not enough of another. Shame is often referred to as the *master emotion* because it modulates and interferes with other emotions so that we don't take action.

Our survival as a species relates to the fact that we are the most social of all animals. Humans have the longest childhood, and we're the most dependent on our parents and society to survive and thrive. As children, we are unlikely to make it without caretakers and a system of support around us. Even as adults, we still need connection with others, not only for happiness, but for our long-term survival. All of this to say that shame is a social emotion.

Shame is designed to help us navigate society's rules and customs so we have a better chance of survival. In this way, shame is meant to keep us out of trouble with others, and few of us would be comfortable in a shameless society, where everybody did whatever they wished with no regard for the feelings and needs of others. A little bit of shame then keeps us in line. Shame reminds us where the boundaries are.

Unfortunately, society's rules aren't always logical, known, compassionate, or understood. Additionally, shame thrives on difference. We're all unique in our own way, but if our differences aren't resolved in a healthy way with others, societal shaming occurs as a result.

## THE DIFFERENCE BETWEEN SHAME AND GUILT

People often ask us about the distinction between shame and guilt. For us, the two are quite different. Guilt is localized—it refers to feeling bad about something you did. Shame, on the other hand, is global— you're convinced that you are bad, defective, and unworthy of love and belonging. Guilt is more cognitive; shame is felt in the body.

Guilt involves agency, as in *I did something wrong that needs to be fixed*. Shame feels powerless. For many, shame feels like a cloak or an ooze that's put on them, or an unfixable hole or wound deep inside. Developmentally, guilt comes later than shame because guilt involves a developed sense of right and wrong. Shame is a primary emotion with us from birth; guilt is secondary.

Western society has shame about shame—feeling shame and talking about it are often viewed as shameful. In part, this book is about countering that view. By understanding the purpose of shame, as well as how it works and affects us, we can begin to look at it with curiosity and learn to appreciate the information it can provide us.

Guilt, on the other hand, is a socially acceptable emotion. People are often proud of their guilt; it's evidence that they're good and moral. Perhaps because of this, many people use the word *guilt* when they really mean *shame*. They may be saying, "I did something wrong, and I feel guilty," when what they really mean (and what they feel inside) is "I did something wrong. That shows that I'm bad, flawed, defective, and unworthy."

## *Sheila's Childhood Shyness*

In high school, I felt so shy and embarrassed that I was often scared of talking to other kids. Even so, when I saw a sign for a workshop to learn how to become a peer counselor, I felt the call. Although my shyness was profoundly painful back then, the part of me that wanted to help others was there too. I imagined how to talk to someone who came for counseling. I could imagine the scenes and my ability to help them. In reality, I couldn't do the partner practices in the training workshop because I was afraid of all the eye contact and felt embarrassed doing the revealing exercises. But later on in life, those scenes I'd imagined in which I was helpful to others guided me to become a therapist.

## RESPONDING TO SHAME

Although we teach about shame all the time, we still have trouble dealing with it at times. You probably do too. Most people try to stay as far away as possible from noticing and exploring shame, but establishing a healthy relationship with shame requires us to approach and understand it.

There are two major ways that people respond to too much shame. First, people can get lost in it. They know they have shame because it's overwhelming and it makes their life hard, but they don't know what to do about it. Second are the people who don't even know they have shame. They might act in ways that are peculiar or in ways they may not understand (and certainly in ways people around them don't understand) because they're reacting against their shame or denying it. They're not in touch with the shame that underlies so much of their behavior.

Because everybody experiences shame in some measure, we want to give you a roadmap to help you navigate shame in a way that gives you a sense of being okay with it. We want to help you be able to look right at the shame and deal with it so shame will just be part of your life and not something that completely blocks or freezes you—not something that you feel compelled to avoid. This is a difficult task because shame is like the many-headed Hydra of Greek mythology. Dealing with all of those heads is a challenging but doable task.

## SHAME SIGNALS AND SHAME SPIRALS

Let's take a look at some of the ways shame manifests and the signals that indicate when shame is present. This can give you a new understanding of what happens to you and to the people around you when shame comes into the picture.

When we feel shame, we don't feel like relating. We either pull in to protect ourselves or push others away. Shame is at the root of the inner critic and perfectionism, and it binds with other emotions, like anger and fear, so it is often hard to detect. Unhealed shame may be a major contributor to depression, eating disorders, addictions, domestic violence, bullying, narcissism, and other dynamics that can get in the way of healthy relationships with ourselves and others. Understanding shame indicators will shed light on some of the blind spots of your thoughts, feelings, and actions.

### A Student Describes Shame

For me, it's a deep sense of not being worthy associated with my muscles tensing and a loss of awareness about my body. It's difficult to stay focused and keep my attention on the group. My heart races, my breathing quickens when it's my turn to speak, it's hard to remember what I wanted to say, and it's difficult to think critically and with much depth. I carry the legacy of shame for my family—from my mother to my grandmother and on up the line. I desperately needed love, attunement, curiosity, and warmth. I was like a spore that had decided it needed to go into survival mode until there were more viable conditions. I just needed a little warmth and tender care to be able to flourish and believe that I was worth making better decisions for myself. ☀

Some people experience shame instantly. They start to hear what sounds like their own voice putting themselves down. Other people might get flashbacks of abuse or horrible memories and then go into a shame freeze and shut down. For others, shame may come up in a less obvious way, with a subtle discomfort in which they feel the need to change the subject, drop a project without knowing why, or suddenly break a promise. For others, it can come up as defensiveness or a stony silence meant to hide the shame.

## COMMON SHAME INDICATORS

Here are some common markers that could be clues that you're experiencing shame:

- **Thoughts:** *There's something wrong with me. I'm a failure. I can't do anything right.*

- **Sensations:** Feeling shy or uncomfortable in your body, having a flushed face, experiencing trouble breathing, having trouble maintaining eye contact.

- **Reactions:** Blaming others, going blank or freezing, using an activity to numb out, disassociating, withdrawing.

## SOME SHAME SPIRAL EXAMPLES

These are a few examples of how shame can quickly spiral away from us:

- Someone's boss sends them an urgent email that says, "I need to talk to you this afternoon, meet me in my office." The person doesn't know what it's about, but immediately starts wondering what they did wrong. Physically, they get flushed, and it feels like their heart is stuck to the bottom of the floor. When they show up to the meeting, they're distracted and worried about their job. But then the boss says, "I appreciate the extra time and extra shifts you do, so I'd like you to take the lead while I'm gone next week." The person sighs with relief, but because they've been putting themself down and worrying so much, it's hard for them to feel happy about the boss's trust in them. Instead, they shame themself for even thinking they were in trouble in the first place.

- A father feels bad that he can't afford to send his son on a trip that all his son's friends are going on. Instead of explaining that to his son, he abruptly puts the kid down for not doing his chores around the house, saying "You're asking for too much!" and "Money doesn't grow on trees!" The son feels ashamed for asking and also ashamed for not being able to go along with his friends. Hurt, the two of them avoid each other for a couple of days, and the isolation only adds to the shame that each feels.

- A woman is out on a date with her new girlfriend. She got a haircut earlier in the day—one she thought looked nice—but her date doesn't seem to notice anything different about her. She begins to shut down, thinking to herself, *What's wrong with me? Why do I always pick insensitive people like this?* Meanwhile, her girlfriend notices the growing silence between them, experiences it as coldness, and begins to pull away, thinking, *This always happens to me. After a couple of dates, they always lose interest and break up with me.*

The common theme of these examples is the running commentary of *something is wrong with me.* Even if that message comes across in a subtle whisper, it's something that contributes to what we believe and feel in a given situation. The commentary about ourselves going on in the background prevents us from being proactive and asking vulnerable questions in order to gain the clarity that might help us receive counter-shaming messages instead.

Because everybody has a slightly different view of the world, what we believe is happening in social situations and what others see happening are often quite different. Even minor misconnections, subtle or unsubtle, can leave us feeling ignored, insulted, or misunderstood, and these often result in increased feelings of shame.

Shame spirals can begin with feeling powerless in a situation, which kicks off self-critical thoughts, which then lead to actions based on those thoughts. But shame can also begin with actions (forgetting our partner's birthday), which then lead to thoughts (*I blew it*), to a feeling of powerlessness, and then to more critical thoughts (*I can't do it right, I can never do it right*).

If you are aware of what's happening, it's possible to stop these cycles and keep yourself out of the shame loop. But a lot of people aren't even aware of their shame, so they keep going round and round with their feelings, thoughts, and responses in unhealthy ways that continue to spiral. And that's the problem with shame—if unaddressed, it tends to spiral.

## THE SECRET CONVERSATIONS OF SHAME

As we hinted at above, shame regularly involves secret, internal conversations with ourselves. Because these conversations happen on a continuum of shame, they can feel different for different people. This is all the stuff people don't talk about. Shame is tricky and can often be so subtle or invisible that most people don't even realize they are feeling these things or having these conversations at all. As you read the examples below, notice what's familiar and remember to be kind and gentle with yourself as you do. Don't take any of it on and don't beat yourself up if any of it feels painfully familiar.

- **Self-conscious** conversations include internal messages such as *Everybody thinks I'm weird, I'm so different from everybody else*, and *I hate it when people stare at me.*

- **Concerned** conversations might sound like *What if I made a mistake?, Maybe I'm in the wrong place,* or *What happens if I blow it?*

- **Judgmental** conversations involve phrases like *It's all my fault, That should never have happened,* or *Somebody around here is to blame.*

- **Rejected** conversations sound more like *Nobody cares about me, I'm alone,* or *I don't matter.*

- **Powerless** conversations may include messages such as *It's out of my control, It's hopeless, Nothing ever changes,* and so on.

These secret conversations are endless. They can be tinted with embarrassment, intense discomfort, a sense of invisibility, feeling stupid or stuck or frozen, laziness, a sense of being fundamentally flawed, humiliation, and more.

Shame can feel painful and crippling, but there's hope. There is a way to transform shame into something that's useful and helpful, and there's a way to transform society so shame becomes a lot more useful and helpful than it normally is. That's the purpose of this book. We want to help you transform your shame. If enough people do that, society's relationship to shame will change too.

To that end, we'd like to close this chapter with some practices to help you change your relationship with shame in a positive way. You'll continue to find practices like these throughout the book. Find the ones that work best for you and remember to be kind to yourself as you explore them.

## PRACTICES

### Grounding

Through gravity, our bodies are connected to the earth. Engaging in grounding exercises can help us in times of disorientation and emotional upset, which can regularly come up as we talk about shame and its associated memories. One grounding practice is to simply breathe at your own pace, pay attention to how your breath enters and exits your body, and allow your out-breath to last just a little longer than the in-breath.

## Pride Visualization

Like other practices you'll come across in this book, this is a meditation and journaling exercise. Grab a notebook or a piece of paper and a pen. Start by noticing your breathing—in and out—inhaling and exhaling at your own pace. Allow yourself to remember a time when you felt proud of something and do your best to call up the memory in detail. Let yourself feel into the pride and all the sensations that come up for you. Continue to breathe at your own pace. After a while, bring your attention back to the present moment and list two to ten kind things people say about you when you are at your best.

2

# Unlocking Shame Binds

*We call shame the master emotion . . . Shame plays a*
*central role in regulating the expression, and indeed, the*
*awareness of all of our other emotions . . . One can be*
*so ashamed of one's emotions that they can be repressed*
*almost completely.*

—Thomas Scheff and Suzanne Retzinger

One of the great insights of Silvan Tomkins, the father of modern shame theory, is that shame is a *binding* emotion. Shame works by binding with and interfering with other emotions. The fact that shame binds with emotions and feeling states is a major reason why shame is so powerful and so hard to track and heal.

Shame is designed to keep us out of trouble by lowering the intensity of other emotions and hampering our tendency to complete their associated behaviors (for example, grieving, reaching out to others, or setting boundaries). When shame binds with anger, fear, joy, curiosity, or grief, those emotions cannot complete themselves, and we can become caught in a maze of feelings with no end. Emotions are designed to move through us and then leave. In fact, the word *emotion* comes from the Latin word *emovere*, which means "move out," "move away," or "remove."

We're meant to experience various emotions, have them affect us for a while, and then feel other emotions in turn. It's like a magician drawing a string of multicolored handkerchiefs from their sleeve or hat, one following the other in a smooth progression. But when shame binds with an emotion, the magic of the human emotional system stops working. It gets stuck. And that's how we get trapped in shame.

The action tendency of shame is to freeze, hide, and disappear. When shame freezes us, we can't access the natural healthy action impulses of our other emotions, like anger, grief, and fear. When primary emotions get subdued, stasis sets in, resulting in confusion and diminished vitality. To make matters even more challenging, knowing that we're not living with the joy and vitality we want to have brings us even more shame. For this reason, it's important to learn how to untangle shame from the other primary emotions so they can complete and we can live in a fuller, more productive, and more joyful way.

## SHAME WITH JOY OR PLEASURE

This is a shame bind that most of us are familiar with. When shame interrupts joy or pleasure, we feel like the wind has been taken out of our sails. When shame is persistent, there's little room for joy or pleasure in the first place. We might start feeling good about something, then feel guilty about that (remember that *guilt* is a more acceptable word for *shame*), so we stop doing what gives us pleasure. Or we continue, but without much satisfaction. Some people may sabotage their pleasure, starting a fight with a close friend or going on a restrictive diet when there's not much reason to. Or they accomplish something important, and rather than savor the moment and celebrate the win, they rush on to the next challenge or thing they have to do. And there's always a next thing to do.

> Shame can bind with any emotion or feeling state.

For most of us, this process starts in childhood, when we can get shamed for giggling or being too exuberant or beginning to explore our sexuality. Silvan Tomkins says that the trigger for innate shame is the "interruption of excitement or joy." Imagine two young sisters jumping up and down on their beds having a blast, laughing and screaming with joy. The noise bothers their mother, who marches in with a stern "Cut it out! I can't hear myself think!" The girls stop their play, hang their heads, lie down, and remain quiet. Without realizing it, the mom has shamed her daughters for simply being kids and having fun. This is one example of how pleasure becomes bound with shame.

## PLEASURE, SHAME, AND ADDICTION

When shame binds with and destroys the ability to enjoy the normal pleasures of life, people will search desperately for something that will give them pleasure or at least relief from the pain or numbness they feel. When they find something that accomplishes that, they can fixate on it and become addicted. The drive for pleasure is now focused solely on one substance or behavior to the exclusion of everything else.

There have been some famous experiments in which rats were isolated and put in a cage with two levers they could press. One lever would dispense food; the other a drug that affected the pleasure centers of the brain. Over time, the rats became more addicted and began to press only the drug-producing lever. They eventually died of starvation. This was seen as proof of the relentlessness of addiction and how powerful drugs can be.

However, a more recent experiment led by Bruce Alexander revealed different results. In Alexander's work, known as *Rat Park*, rats were not isolated in cages but were placed in a "rat park" with lots of other rats. The rats could play, fight, have sex, and connect in all the ways that rats like to do. They were offered drugs in this experiment; only in this case, the rats gradually lost interest, and not a single rat became addicted.[1]

Just as rats need activity and other rats to be happy, people need people. When shame disrupts our ability to gain pleasure from being active or to connect with others, we become more prone to addiction. This is especially true when the shame comes from physical or emotional deprivation in childhood.

While the joy-shame (or pleasure-shame) bind is well-known, shame can bind with any emotion or feeling state. When bound in shame, we lack the resources to follow through on the appropriate action tendency of that emotion, which disconnects us and hinders our ability to take care of ourselves by acting appropriately.

## SHAME AND ANGER

We believe shame was originally (in other words evolutionarily) designed to lessen the impact of anger because anger can get us into a lot of social trouble. If we lash out at others, or even complain to the wrong people, we can face consequences. This is particularly true for children and the adults who look after them. Shame is nature's way of keeping us safe by lowering the emotion of anger, but often to the extent that a lot of people aren't in touch with their anger. Or if they feel it, they're ashamed of it, which keeps them from acting on it.

Culturally, far too many of us are uneasy and unskilled with anger. Anger has a bad name in our society because we associate it with violence. But anger is a natural response to injustice, and anger is what helps us set boundaries. The action tendency of anger is to change something. Anger arises spontaneously in children when they don't get what they want or when they are subject to something unpleasant. Unfortunately, our societal unease and avoidance of anger leave most of us estranged from and unskilled with the emotion.

Mahatma Gandhi, traveling on a first-class ticket, was kicked out of a railway car in South Africa because a white passenger complained. Gandhi spent the night shivering in the unheated railway station waiting room.

The incident led to his creation of *satyagraha*, what became widely known as "passive resistance." People mistakenly believe that Gandhi preached nonviolence, but *satyagraha* actually means something closer to "standing up for yourself" because Gandhi believed in a form of righteous anger that empowers us to stand up for what's right.[2] Shame binds with (and interferes with) that righteous anger.

Anger is connected to our life force. It arises because something matters to us. Anger acknowledges that what we feel, think, and want is important, and it provides the energy for us to take action. Anger comes up when we want something we're not getting as well as when we get something we don't want. While we need to be able to channel our anger, as Gandhi did, shame can get in the way of taking useful action.

## SHAME AND GRIEF

When shame binds with grief, it doesn't allow the grief to complete. The action tendency of grief is to cry and seek solace. Ideally you grieve, mourn, receive comfort, weep, do whatever else you need to do, and eventually move through it. You may feel the grief intensely for a long time, often much longer than our society allows for, but it will eventually fade or transform.

It's normal and appropriate to feel grief about past losses. Unfortunately, we are often shamed for carrying our grief too long, for feeling grief on the anniversaries of a loss, or when the losses that affect us seem minor to others. Too often, the support or guidance we receive is all about gaining control over ourselves. This produces a grief-shame bind, in which we still feel the grief, but we also feel shame on top of it. Sometimes we feel additional shame because we feel in some way responsible for the loss.

Grief is designed so that we receive comfort for our losses and eventually move beyond them. Shame, however, keeps everything in a perpetual present. In Western culture, we are set up for the grief-shame bind through a bias for power and control. By extolling success, happy thoughts, and control, we receive social or cultural shame about grieving loss and helplessness because grieving is viewed as weak. This easily becomes shame upon shame. Shame at the loss. Shame for not knowing what to do. Shame for having shame. We end up with a collage of losses and shame that accumulate, for most of us, over a lifetime.

### A Student Reflects on Shame and Grief

It has been shocking to me to recognize how much shame I have coupled with other suppressed emotions. I never realized how much shame I have about my suppressed grief from losses in my life. In realizing that I was conditioned to be ashamed of my grief, I have also realized that that shame has prevented me from processing a lifetime of painful losses.

People often feel that they could have prevented losses if only they'd thought, acted, or prayed differently. That shame adds to the shame of grieving for longer than is approved. The shame of not having done the right thing, or not having done enough, is especially acute when the loss involves death. Much of Western society sees death as the ultimate limitation that we face (which it is) and also as the ultimate failure (which it isn't). Because we generally don't want to be reminded of our powerlessness over death, people who are grieving can be shamed and told to get over it. As one student reported, "When I was processing my father's death, someone got impatient with my suddenly breaking into tears, out of control, and responded, 'Jeez, it's been three weeks.'"

The standard number of bereavement days offered by employers borders on ludicrous. Timetables on grief demean the experience of loss, and the absence of widespread rituals to help us process grief does us all a disservice. Rituals validate the experience of loss and the complexity of grief and offer ways to move through this human experience. Without these rituals, people are unsupported in a barrage of confusion and uncertainty. Confusion breeds shame; shame breeds confusion. This seems especially true in the shame-laden context of a loss as substantial as death.

Mourning helps us to grieve and move on, and grief helps us change from who we were in the past. Shame keeps us frozen and anchored to past events, which means we remain in a perpetual present, which then keeps us in shame. And if the shame is bound with grief, that means we're always in grief.

No matter the relationship, there's always unfinished business when it comes to the end. It's normal to feel like we should have done more, should have been a better child or sibling or friend, should have prevented someone from dying, should be grieving more or differently. Feelings of shame are more likely when the relationship was a difficult one and produced ambivalent feelings. For example, when a child feels both anger and grief at a lack of connection with their parent—a sense of not being met. Those feelings become even more powerful and confusing when the parent dies.

### Susan and Her Mother

In one workshop session, we worked with a student who was having trouble coming to terms with her mother's death. Susan had always wanted more from her relationship with her mother. It seemed her siblings were content with the depth of connection, but Susan felt unmet in her desire to be seen and cared for by her mother. Susan had invested a lot, both emotionally and financially, in trying to help her mother learn about physical and emotional health, but things didn't change much. And her mother died unexpectedly at age seventy-four.

During the session, it became clear to Susan that her mother was not on board for changing her habits. And that even though they had been working on their emotional closeness, overall, her mother was content with how things were. She was fine with the way she had lived her life—even if it brought on a sudden death! Considering this, Susan changed her tone. She no longer sounded confused. "Let's tell the truth," she said. "The intimacy I was longing for from my mother wasn't going to happen. I was signed up for it, but she wasn't. From her point of view, she felt I was always pressuring her to do things she didn't want to do." With that realization, Susan teared up, "It's embarrassing to give up and admit that I can't fix it. Even if she had lived much longer, I couldn't have fixed it." All of us were deeply affected by the session, feeling the profundity and truth of where Susan had arrived.

We are limited human beings. With life comes loss, no matter how good, powerful, or careful we are. We can't fix death, and there are no perfect goodbyes. Remembering this can help us melt the grief-shame bind.

## SHAME AND FEAR

Fear and shame are part of our powerful human inheritance oriented to safety and belonging. Shame and fear feed on each other. The fear-shame bind activates high affect along with immobility. Fear is designed to protect us from the threat of being physically harmed or killed. Shame is meant to keep us from being rejected and abandoned by the people we need to help us stay alive and connected.

Fear involves a temporary freeze as we reassess the situation and try to locate the source of threat. When a deer hears a rustle in the bushes, it stops moving. Its ears zero in on the sound, and it looks for the source to determine if there's a threat. If so, the freeze gives way to flight—it runs away. The action tendency of shame is to hide and disappear in place, to vanish rather than run away. Although an older deer will run away, a young fawn can't possibly escape like that, so its survival mechanism is to freeze. At birth, fawns don't have much scent, so the freeze works. The predator doesn't see or smell it.

In humans, the temporary freeze of fear and the more permanent freeze of shame reinforce each other. The action tendency of flight conflicts with the action tendency of disappearing in place, and the two go round and round in an ever-tightening spiral. When children feel fear, they often seek comfort and reassurance, but children (especially boys) are sometimes shamed by parents and peers for showing or expressing fear. Getting this reaction, a child may decide that fear is unreasonable and unwelcome, and they may not realize that others feel fear also. They begin to hide their fear to keep connected to family and friends and then become even more afraid that people will find out they are afraid. This is how fear gets bound with shame.

## A Student's Fear-Shame Bind

What I have understood to be anxiety for my entire life has actually been shame. I can see that my various issues in life all connect to a core shame wound: chronic back tension, migraines, anxiety of all kinds, feeling especially anxious and self-conscious in groups, the sense that I am stupid, body-image issues, and not feeling good enough in most respects. I also learned that shame is a combination of a primary emotion and a state of freeze—for me, the classic fear-shame bind. And if the action tendency of fear is to flee or run away, is that why I have been so drawn to running—a source of pride, freedom, and mastery, *plus* a way that I can fulfill my action tendency? It is where I have been able to tap into my emotions, often crying or feeling an incredible upwelling of joy and gratitude. I wonder if this is because it is a space where my shame is lowered enough to allow the emotions to come forth and to completion.

The statement that shame makes you stupid resonates deeply with me. I have often felt stupid when in front of others, not able to formulate thoughts and think of words, et cetera. I used to think that I was not smart enough or worthy of people's time. I concluded that it was because I was socially anxious, but now I am understanding that I am deeply ashamed. The source of my anxiety is shame and the fear of being perceived negatively or being seen for who my shamed part wants me to believe that I am. As I am speaking or being observed, I simultaneously think of how people must be critiquing my appearance, my words, and my abilities. It's unbearable at times. ☀

In studying shame binds, we've come to think of trauma as basically an extreme fear-shame bind. While the fear is extreme and very present, shame is always there as well, perpetuating and increasing the freeze. We believe, along with others, that trauma is not what happens to you, but how you react to it. The most intense moment of the trauma experience is actually a moment of shame.

## PERFORMANCE ANXIETY

Public speaking is often cited as a common fear of people from the United States. For some people, it's even more terrifying than the fear of death. When people report that they're frightened of speaking in public, what they're truly afraid of is being shamed. When we say we have *stage fright*, we're focusing on the fear part of the experience without paying attention to the shame aspect. The therapeutic term for stage fright is *performance anxiety*, which is all about being humiliated, laughed at, judged, ignored, or disliked. In other words, it's about being shamed. Performance anxiety is related to *social anxiety*: feeling uncomfortable in groups, not wanting to attend parties, avoiding interacting with others, and so on. This is also commonly referred to as shyness. It's the same fear-shame bind: a fear of being shamed, a fear of being made fun of or harshly critiqued in some way. If we leave out the shame portion of the bind, we miss what the experience is about. Worse, we can't successfully heal it.

### A Therapist Solves Her Own Problem
*Shame causes us to completely focus on ourselves.* I remember having this realization immediately before I saw my first client eight years ago, but of course I didn't know it was shame at the time, rather I thought of it as *my anxiety*. I remember being incredibly worried about how I was going to do, if I was going to mess up, if I would freeze and not know what to say—the thoughts were ruminative and led to me feeling paralyzed. About an hour before she was scheduled to arrive, I had this light bulb moment where I realized that every concern I had was about myself and

my performance. I was shocked and immediately lowered into another layer of shame about this pattern. Fortunately, I was able to pivot my attention to the client's experience. I started wondering how the client may be feeling about coming in for therapy and what they may need from me. By thinking about my new client's feelings, and not just my own, I rebuilt the interpersonal bridge between us in my mind. I had been on an isolated and terrifying island all by myself. This quickly calmed my system to a more manageable and normal level of anxiety that a new therapist would feel upon meeting with her first client.

With our student's shame no longer binding with her fear, the spiral was broken, and she only had to handle a manageable level of anxiety. But without acknowledging the inner shame bind of not feeling good enough and creating that new bridge within herself and with her client, she would have remained in a shame freeze. She would have had limited access to higher-level thinking and language skills, fulfilled her fears, and then created a new shame-based story about her capabilities based on the state of her nervous system, not her actual skills.

## THE IMPOSTER SYNDROME

The imposter syndrome is an important manifestation of the fear-shame bind. It happens when someone feels inadequate at their job or their position in life and is afraid of being found out as lacking, of being exposed for the lesser person they believe they truly are. We see this play out in the famous story "The Emperor's New Clothes." Having been bamboozled by hucksters, the emperor in the tale appears in public totally naked, wearing only the imaginary clothes that he has bought from the con artists. That vision of being naked and exposed in public is the essence of shame.

We all have moments of feeling like imposters and unworthy of any honors or of feeling that we're inadequate in our work. The embodied messages are along the lines of: *I'm a fraud. I'm not competent enough to do this job, even if people think I am. Eventually, they'll discover the truth, and I'll be revealed as a fake. I'll be fired, insulted, or laughed at. I'm completely unable to live up to the role, responsibility, or beliefs that others have about me.* We feel shame in the moment, perhaps historic shame from the last time something went wrong, and then a combination of fear and anticipatory shame as we imagine future rejection and humiliation. And because fear and shame freeze the mind and body, we stumble. We perform poorly. That poor performance thus confirms our shame and our belief that we are not up for the job. We may begin to judge the past as well, thinking that we have always been a fraud and we never belonged in the first place. Shame doubles down, and fear layers with shame at the performances that do not fulfill expectations (internal or external), which lowers our performance level even more.

Even if we manage to perform well despite all this and are praised for doing a good job, the praise is lost in the self-criticism that rages inside of us, and our fear prevails. We tell ourselves, *I may have gotten away with it this time, but they'll eventually find out.*

## Sheila's High School Memory

When I was in high school, I found that getting to science class early felt rewarding because I got to be the one to help the teacher set up the experiments before the class started. I was a little less shy each time. Then the teacher announced to the class that I was to be his lab assistant for the class. I remember glowing with a little hint of pride and self-esteem, and I was able to enjoy those feelings for a couple months. But then I started to have doubts. *What if I make a mistake on the next experiment?* I worried. *What if I hook the positive end to the negative end? What if I put the little beaker where the big beaker should be? What if I'm really a fraud?* If I made a mistake, everyone would see I was a failure. My terrible hidden shyness came rushing back, and it became so bad that I actually got sick one day and missed the class. What had been an opportunity to transform my shyness became just another place where I came down on myself and convinced myself that I couldn't do it right.

At the next class, the teacher asked me why I was absent, and I confided my doubts to him: I was worried about messing an experiment up, about making a mistake. I can still remember hearing his comforting voice say: "We'll do it together. And if you have questions, just ask." And then he said these magic words: "That's what practice is for!" That became sort of like a mantra for me that I could repeat before class and at other times during my day. There were all sorts of places in life where I needed practice! Remembering that, I was able to go back to being a lab assistant and not worrying about mistakes so much. I could hear my teacher's kind reassuring voice, and eventually, I was able to hear my own kind voice too. It was one of those formative experiences that made me want to become a teacher and a therapist.

## THE COMPLEXITY OF SHAME-BOUND EMOTIONS

Every shame bind has layers of fear, anger, and sadness—fear of rejection, desire for belonging, and anger and grief from the historic breaking of the interpersonal bridge. One of the more fascinating aspects of shame binds is how many emotions get involved. When we experience important events in our lives, various emotions come up at the same time. Depending on childhood conditioning, certain emotions are considered desirable; others are not. We tend to avoid the emotions that were not okay to feel in childhood; these get bound with shame and often stay hidden from us. We typically only experience the emotions that were acceptable.

### Jennine's Story

I realized how grief from my past circumstances is bound up with or masked as fears about the future. I now have a new revelation about how shame, grief, and fear can all be bound up together. I think that fear is a less vulnerable emotion than grief and additionally feels more empowering because I feel like I have more control over my life when I think about what I can do to prevent my fears, while there isn't much I can *do* about the things in the past for which I'm grieving. As a person who is obsessed with productivity and control over my life, I tend to be more future leaning than past leaning. I don't want to waste time feeling sad about the past. I want to do something about avoiding the same problems in the future! Unconsciously, I think overriding sadness with fear made me feel like I was doing something to avoid pain in the future, but in hindsight, I think it was more there to mask the sadness, and more times than not, it didn't actually lead me to any productive action because it was oftentimes bound up with shame.

As much as I've been taught how important it is for emotions to complete, I have historically struggled to embrace the value of spending time in sadness or grief. When I was in my first trimester of pregnancy and feeling insanely exhausted, perpetually nauseous, and incredibly vulnerable all around, I couldn't suppress my grief or channel it into falsely empowering fear the way I'm usually able to. After an individual session with Bret, I realized there was grief inside of me that I had been holding onto, and I made space for myself to grieve, per his instruction. In the session, he helped me disentangle the shame from the grief, which helped me to move through that grief. As much as it was difficult to let the flood of emotions surface, both around grieving the loss of my idyllic, free, childless life and around grieving what could have been in my relationship with my partner—had he not been going through and reacting out of his own shame through many years of our marriage—I felt a cathartic release after discovering my grief, acknowledging it, and crying it out with the support of friends, therapists, and my community.

In Jennine's family of origin, sadness was not okay. Most of the focus was on doing well in school and preparing for success in the future. It was okay to fear the future, but not to grieve the past. In your childhood, the acceptable emotions and the ones you were taught to be ashamed of might have been different. There are endless variations, and shame takes advantage of all of them.

## SHAME AND DEPRESSION

Depression has become an epidemic in the Western world. While depression is often equated with sadness, it is actually an absence of feelings and vitality—an emotional deadness. One theory states that depression is anger turned in against the self. The depressed person can't get angry at others, so they turn it inward.

We see depression as the result of a complex anger-grief-fear-shame bind. It's a stew of emotions, all bound by shame. Depression is an extreme withdraw reaction to all-pervasive shame. The shame around the emotions is so intense that the person gives up on life and gives in to hopelessness and despair—the sisters of shame. In order to help someone with depression, we need to unbind the shame so we can free up life force.

## SHAME AND CURIOSITY

Curiosity is hardwired into the human brain. Silvan Tomkins lists curiosity as one of nine primary emotions.[3] We believe that curiosity is the most distinctively human emotion there is. While most animals are interested in new objects or other animals they encounter, humans are distinctly curious about everything. Our need to explore and understand our world is the quality that's led us to populate the planet and eventually (for better or worse) become the dominant species.

> Curiosity is an antidote to shame.

When our curiosity is piqued, the parts of the brain that regulate pleasure and reward light up. There's a basic neural circuit that energizes us to go out and get things that are intrinsically rewarding. This circuit lights up when we get money or candy as well as when we engage our curiosity. When the circuit is activated, our brains release dopamine, which gives us pleasure, satisfaction, and motivation. Dopamine also seems to play a role in enhancing the connections between cells involved in learning.

Children delight in exploring their surroundings, but the more shame we encounter as we age, the more our gaze turns inward, and we lose interest and contact with the world around us. We develop tunnel vision. The more shame we have, the more we become rigid in our thinking and behavior and the less curiosity we have. In fact, low curiosity and high rigidity are indicators of shame. We stop wondering and exploring and believe we already have all the answers we need as a way of self-protection.

Interestingly enough, curiosity is an antidote to shame. We can begin to heal shame if we become curious about our situation, about what's happening around us, about what happened in the past, about what's going on for other people. When we activate our curiosity in this way, our brain comes to life again, our vision expands, and we melt the shame freeze and start functioning better. Curiosity emerges when shame is unbound from fear and creativity.

Curiosity is a sign that someone is coming out of freeze. It's also an indicator that the ventral vagal nerve—which controls social engagement and connection with the world—is coming back online. This is the opposite of shame and trauma.

### A Client Gets Curious

Just the other day, a client who has been in my office more than a dozen times looked at a very large painting on the wall right next to her chair and asked if it was new. She then expressed embarrassment when I disclosed that in fact it has been there for years. But as with any client who discovers something old in my office for the first time, I was able to counter-shame her by inserting the education piece and indicating that her noticing the painting was a good thing—a sign that she's coming out of freeze and able to bask a bit, be relaxed enough to orient, to notice, and to be curious about her surroundings, to be less hypervigilant.

When we work with clients or students, we always use our compassionate curiosity to ask questions both to find out where the shame comes from and to find out what resources the client has available to them. In doing this, we try to evoke the curiosity of the client and open their mind so they can see a bigger picture. For example, we often work with clients who have the strong belief that everyone in their family is against them, but when we explore their extended family system with curiosity, we usually find at least one person who is on their side.

If you can be compassionate with yourself and harness your curiosity, if you can notice your surroundings, and if you can become interested in what's going on for other people, you can begin to emerge from shame. The key is curiosity with caring, relatedness, and compassion.

## PRACTICES

### Unlocking Shame Binds

For any of the three unlocking practices below (for the grief-shame bind, the anger-shame bind, and the pleasure-shame bind), please start with this short grounding exercise:

Feel your feet on the floor and breathe at your own pace for a while. At some point, see if you can make the out-breath last just a little longer than the in-breath. Place your hand on your heart and tell yourself, *This breath is all I need to observe but not react.*

Let yourself breathe for a few minutes. With your hand on your heart, say, *This courage is all I need right now.* Take another breath and imagine that above your head, a string connects you to the sky and pulls you up. Then imagine there's a string under you that connects you to the ground and pulls your energy safely to the earth.

Breathe in the energy of courage and breathe out the messiness of shame binds. Breathe in courage and breathe out shame. You don't have to fix anything. Just notice the thoughts and feelings that have been coming up as you've been reading about shame binds and thinking about your life.

## For the Grief-Shame Bind

Think about something you feel grief about. Have you lost someone you couldn't save? Did someone think unkindly about you? Do you have any grief about what you have lost in life? Let yourself freewrite using the following prompts:

> I notice . . .
>
> I also notice . . .
>
> I wish I could have changed . . .
>
> I can't let go of feeling . . .
>
> I wish I could tell someone . . .

After you've written on these prompts for a while (or anything else that comes up), tell yourself, *I hear you now. I am here with you now. I care about your feelings.*

## For the Anger-Shame Bind

Is there something you feel angry about? Have you told yourself that you have to keep this anger inside? Was there anger you had to hold back to protect your family or others? Take a few minutes and let yourself write a few lines as above:

> I notice . . .
>
> I also notice . . .
>
> I wish I could have changed . . .
>
> I can't let go of feeling . . .
>
> I wish I could tell someone . . .

To conclude, remind yourself once more that all of your feelings are welcome here.

## For the Pleasure-Shame Bind

In what ways do you prevent yourself from fully experiencing pleasure or joy? How does shame get in the way of having fun? How does the shame stop you? As above, use the following prompts to explore this in writing:

> I notice . . .
>
> I also notice . . .
>
> I wish I could have changed . . .
>
> I can't let go of feeling . . .
>
> I wish I could tell someone . . .

Remember to breathe and let yourself know that your feelings are welcome.

To conclude and move on from any of these practices, take a deep breath and shake out your hands several times to release the energy that's been activated. It can also help to stomp your feet several times and say, *I am good enough, and I am letting go of this a little bit at a time.* As always, gently touch in with yourself and ask your deeper self or your higher self or your wise mind what you need in the moment. Do you need to move on to the next chapter? To take a break and rest or replenish yourself? Here and elsewhere in the book, be sure to creatively celebrate your discoveries as you move through these practices.

## 3

# Reactions to Shame

*"Why are you drinking?" demanded the little prince.*
*"So that I may forget," replied the tippler.*
*"Forget what?" inquired the little prince, who already*
*was sorry for him.*
*"Forget that I am ashamed," the tippler confessed,*
*hanging his head.*
*"Ashamed of what?" insisted the little prince, who*
*wanted to help him.*
*"Ashamed of drinking!"*

—Antoine de Saint-Exupéry, *The Little Prince*

O ne of the reasons shame is so powerful is that shame is a master of disguise. Invisibility creates power. If you can't be seen, you are free to do more damage. Often when someone behaves a certain way, we can't see how their behavior is motivated by shame, and even they may not be aware that they feel shame (or that they feel anything at all). Meanwhile, shame is there the entire time, hiding in plain sight.

Because shame is so painful, people avoid feeling it. Therefore, most of what we see in people when they feel shame is not the shame itself, but an unconscious way of reacting to the unbearable feeling of shame in their nervous system. As painful and self-defeating as the reactions may be, they offer some relief from the childhood disruption that triggers them. What we most often see and feel is not the shame itself, but a *reaction* to the shame.

When you start to see shame more clearly and pierce through its disguises, experiences that once seemed mysterious to you will begin making sense. You will come to better understand what is happening for you, as well as for the people you interact with.

Donald Nathanson delineated four main reactions to shame that we've built on over the years.[1] These are unconscious responses people have to avoid feeling the shame that affects their nervous system. Recognizing these reactions as signposts for shame becomes like a Rosetta Stone for understanding people's behavior and what underlies that behavior. When we understand these reactions to shame, a lot of difficult and uncomfortable words and actions suddenly make more sense.

## THE FOUR REACTIONS TO SHAME

There are four main reactions to shame: Attack Self, Attack Other, Deny, and Withdraw. Most people tend to have one of these unconscious reactions when they feel shame. There are any number of factors that can cause us to unconsciously prefer one of these reactions as our go-to: modeling (how our caregivers reacted when they felt shame), media bias (how our favorite heroes and villains express themselves), genetic proclivities (introverts tending to withdraw), and so forth. Some people may ping-pong from reaction to reaction, but shame—and the unconscious motivation to avoid feeling it—underlie them all. Each of these reactions has value and utility. However, when we become stuck in one of these four, we're unable to see or deal with the shame that underlies it.

## Attack Self

The Attack-Self reaction looks a lot like shame itself. Someone is ashamed of their weight or their skin tone or because they didn't do well on a test. They feel ashamed, and it shows. A person might attack themself for not fitting social norms of body size or because someone made fun of them. This reaction feels justified due to society's persistent messages about the importance of physical appearance and "fitting in."

However, shame isn't just the product of our present experience. Certainly, there are experiences of trauma and public humiliation that can produce intense present shame, but in most cases, an intense level of shame is actually a sign of a childhood experience that's being triggered in the nervous system. We call the present occurrence a *shame trigger*. The level of intensity we feel in the moment is related to the degree of shame we experienced in the past. This is the 90/10 Split we referenced in chapter 1.

One common manifestation of Attack Self is the negative self-talk often referred to as the *inner critic*. Classic phrases the inner critic uses are things like *I'm terrible, I always mess up,* and *I deserve it* (whatever the "it" is—insult, punishment, an unfavorable outcome).

### The Inner Critic at Work

*I put myself down before anyone else can. I've made myself late so I don't get promoted, and I intentionally make mistakes so I can disappear sometimes so I won't get noticed. Some people know there's something wrong with them. Well, I know nothing's right with me.*

Another form of Attack Self is *perfectionism*. Sometimes people feel so unworthy deep down that the only path forward to a sense of self-worth is to strive for perfection. That's a tall order, considering that nobody can become perfect. And while a little perfectionism can help you do a better job, too much creates problems. As Voltaire shared hundreds of years ago, and as Bret still remembers vividly hearing Spock say in a *Star Trek* episode, "The perfect is the enemy of the good."

## *Bret's Thoughts on "Being Perfect"*

In writing this book, I often felt blocked. The words simply wouldn't come. I knew I had plenty to say, but it's hard to do so in book form—you can't change the words after they're in print, you can't answer questions. . . . I was trying so hard to get every line right. My writing only freed up when we hired an editor because then I knew that I could write whatever I wanted. I told myself that if something was wrong, our editor would fix it, and that became my mantra. My writing didn't have to be perfect anymore. The floodgates opened, and I could write freely.

The advantage of the Attack-Self reaction is that it includes a certain willingness to take responsibility. We want to do the right thing; we want to learn and grow.

## PRACTICE

If you tend to attack yourself, slow down and ask yourself, *If I wasn't beating myself up, what would I be doing right now? What would I want?*

## Attack Other

In Attack Other, shame is externalized as blame. We immediately criticize others as an explanation for the situation that has brought up our shame. We're not the problem; somebody else must be the problem. In this way, shame acts like a hot potato—we have to get it away from us as quickly as possible, whether that means contempt toward others, anger, and—in extreme cases—violence.

Our attacks against others are almost always misdirected. We're usually angry at people and situations from a long time ago, and it's that shame from our past that people in the present have triggered. And because shame leaves us feeling powerless, shifting the attack to other people can give us a sense of power and efficacy. This can be especially true of people who have been conditioned by toxic masculinity because they are socialized to be ashamed of being powerless. Studies of violent offenders invariably find that perpetrators have commonly experienced extreme shaming incidents in childhood. These people might be aware of what happened to them in the past, but they're not able to deal with it in any other way than inflicting harm upon others. Of course, most of us don't go to that extreme. We merely become angry, hypercritical, and express contempt.

### Bret Versus the Rock

I was careless and tripped on a rock recently. I immediately blamed the rock and had some choice words to say to it. And while the rock probably didn't mind, I have found myself criticizing others, including Sheila, far more often than I would like. It's important that I be aware of my tendency to Attack Other and consciously choose to hold my tongue or take a walk before I speak so I can calm down.

If we're able to calm down and control our verbal and physical behaviors, the Attack-Other reaction can be useful in setting necessary boundaries. Indeed, we may attack others because we didn't set a boundary soon enough.

## Deny

Denial takes many forms. In one extreme (and maddening) form, we simply don't remember what we said or did in the past. Many people deal with shame by denying and forgetting what actually happened. This includes alcohol or drug blackouts in which a person wakes up the next morning with no memory of what happened. We may also remember but deny that we do.

### Sheila's Naked (and Denying) Patient

One of Sheila's former patients was hospitalized and said, "I don't know why I'm here. I'm not supposed to be here. There's been a mistake, and you should release me." Sheila responded by saying, "Maybe there has been a mistake. Let's take a look at your chart." Sheila checked the man's chart and said, "This is really interesting. Your chart says you're here because the police found you running naked down the freeway at two in the morning, and they picked you up and brought you to the psych hospital. Apparently, that's why you're here." The man claimed to have no memory of the incident.

We can Deny that painful events actually happened, or we can Deny our feelings. Denial can involve disassociation, numbness, and blankness. Denial of shame is a central component in most addictions, whether to drugs, alcohol, food, or sex.

John Bradshaw wrote *Healing the Shame That Binds You* as a recovering alcoholic. In the book, he writes about drinking to mask his feelings of shame. When drunk, Bradshaw would do things he should feel ashamed of without feeling any shame. Then, when he would sober up, the shame would attack again, and he would feel so much shame (both for what he did while drunk and for the drinking itself) that he would immediately drink again to mask the pain.[2] This demonstrates clearly how shame is a central part of the addictive cycle.

Addiction works too well, especially for deniers ("Problem? What problem?"). When people are engaging in their addictions, their mind may calm and problems can seem to magically disappear. But in order to achieve that feeling again, addicts have to drink more, eat more, or work or exercise harder and harder. The more our pain gets denied and pushed down, the more it seems to want to resurface. That leads to us needing yet more of what we're addicted to just to control our shame.

We believe that you can't fully overcome an addiction without working on the shame that underlies it. The success of the Alcoholics Anonymous

(AA) program is related to both the safety that's often created in the AA community and the confrontation and stripping away of habitual denial. People in AA are taught to say, "I am an alcoholic." Even after years of recovery, they will say, "I am a recovering alcoholic"—not "recovered" alcoholic. In this way, they remain mindful and don't let the social shaming that can be directed at alcoholics force them into even more denial.

Of course, we can Deny without having an addiction. We can lose track of details or belongings or misremember conversations or just not feel much of anything at all. Denial can be quite subtle, and we may not realize we're doing it at the time. In some cases, there's a use for denial, especially when we have to act in a crisis and don't have the time or safety to reflect and remain fully aware.

## Fawn/Cling

There is a type of Deny reaction that we believe needs a special mention. We've borrowed this reaction from Pete Walker and have situated it somewhere between Deny and Attack Self, because we view Fawn/Cling as a special form of denial.[3] Just as a deer fawn avoids danger by keeping completely still to avoid detection, the person enacting a Fawn/Cling response freezes inside because it's too unsafe to experience the anger they feel. Often this involves children who need to keep their connection with caregivers, no matter what. We've worked a lot with agencies that sponsor foster and adoptive parents. The adoptive parents often report that children still idolize and long for the parents who gave them up, even if those parents were addicted, abusive, or neglectful. This is the Fawn/Cling reaction at work, and it continues long after it's necessary because the basic need for connection and survival supersedes the reality of the situation.

While there are often social and financial reasons that victims of domestic violence stay in untenable situations, there can also be a Fawn/Cling response that may take over their nervous system. If that happens, they don't have access to a healthy anger, which would get them moving and help them break free, so they freeze. They remain focused on keeping the connection, not allowing themselves to realize or act on the realization that the situation is harmful for them. We also see the Fawn/Cling reaction play out in Stockholm syndrome—a coping mechanism in which people develop positive feelings toward their captors or abusers over time. This condition applies to situations including child abuse, coach-athlete abuse, relationship abuse, and sex trafficking.

Because we live in a male-dominated patriarchal society, the Fawn/Cling reaction is wired into many women developmentally, and it is important for them and others to understand that it is not their fault. It can often protect them in the context of violence. A person attempts to diminish a threat (a physical attack, conflict, criticism, or disapproval) and maintain connection by becoming appealing and abandoning many of their basic needs. Fawn/Cling can also occur in the absence of an overt threat, when a person simply longs for connection with a distant partner or caregiver who is unwilling or unavailable for loving connection.

### Terrence Goes Along to Get Along

When our anger becomes frozen, it's difficult to set boundaries. Terrence was a middle-aged man who had spent most of his life in awkward shyness. At some point, he met a woman, and they eventually developed a serious relationship. Terrence didn't have the courage to ask her to marry him, but he was delighted when she asked him. But Terrence became worried about losing his fiancée, because he'd never told her no or asked for anything. As he explained, his method during dating was to "go along to get along," but now he was afraid that he would have to go along with all of her ideas about the wedding plans and where they would go on their honeymoon. In fact, Terrence was afraid of disagreeing with her about anything. He didn't know how to set a boundary, and he didn't know how to say no. He didn't even know what he wanted until his girlfriend asked for something he didn't want. Terrence had learned this Fawn/Cling reaction as a child, and now he didn't know how to break the pattern. Over time, he learned how to speak up for what he wanted and was better able to set boundaries in the relationship. ✳

## Withdraw

Withdrawal may sound a lot like denial, but it's quite different. In denial, we can stay in a situation and pretend all is well. We may cut off our awareness that the situation is happening (or that our shameful feelings are happening) or use an addictive behavior to dull our awareness, but when we sober up, we can still Deny that we have a problem.

Withdrawal means that we leave the situation physically or emotionally. We pull inward and separate from the shaming situation. Temporary Withdrawal can be useful when it creates some emotional distance and gives us time to calm down. Maybe we take a walk to think about it or take a few minutes to ourselves to review what happened. In a temporary Withdrawal, we can look at the situation in a different way and get a more accurate and helpful take on what's going on. It gives us time to pause, rest, and reassess.

However, for some people, Withdrawal becomes a way of life. They Withdraw permanently and don't come back; they give up on other people and themselves. The shame Withdrawal can easily lead to depression, and we believe that shame is at the root of depression.

### Sheila's Withdrawn Client

I had a young client, Mack, who'd recently dropped out of college and kept to his house. When his worried mother tried to talk with him and get him to go out, he retreated to his bedroom. When I asked him (over Zoom) what he had done that week, he responded, "Absolutely nothing." With further questioning, he admitted that he had worked out. He had a pull-up bar that he could hook up in the doorway. This fascinated me, so I began asking questions. He told me how many reps he could do and that he was increasing the number every day. I was impressed. "I couldn't even do one of these," I told him. Then I asked for his advice on how I could begin to use a pull-up bar, and he gave it willingly. As we talked, he became more animated, and I could see his chest rise and fall as his breathing increased. The beginnings of a smile crossed his lips. He began to come out of his shell. Over time, he was better able to reassess and view himself in a more positive light. Whereas before he'd withdrawn from life because he felt like such a failure, eventually he was able to believe that he could accomplish something worthy and tangible. 🌅

## THE MAGIC OF REASSESSMENT

When it comes to shame, reassessment doesn't always go well. If instead of bringing in tools and techniques for working with the shame, the person goes down a rabbit hole of more self-shaming, they can end up in a compromised emotional state, traveling even further into more isolation and mistrust. They can ultimately lose faith and hope. This is a well-known spiral: the shame initially causes the person to withdraw, the reassessment causes even deeper withdrawal, and the person ends up in an increased shamed state. It's possible, in this state, for that person to flip into one of the other reactions of shame—Attack Self (at worst, a suicide attempt), for example, or Attack Other (violently lashing out at others).

> The result of positive reassessment is *healthy shame.*

If the reassessment goes well, everything can change for the better, as things did for Mack when Sheila helped him. Their discussion about the pull-up bar was only the first step in their work together. One can reassess and come to a different understanding of what happened in the past and of how shame played its part, and come to a different place with it. If you're interested in trying out a reassessment process, we strongly recommend having someone help you. The result of positive reassessment is *healthy shame* (which we'll dive into in the next chapter).

*How Sheila Works with the Reactions to Shame*

There's a chart we use that includes all the reactions to shame covered in this book. I use it to help clients identify their reactions to shame without yet bringing shame up as an underlying factor. In fact, I cover the word *shame* with a sticky note. When they have seen their behaviors and acknowledged them, I might say something like, "There's something else going on here. I wonder if there's a feeling that we haven't identified or talked about yet." Typically, they don't have a guess. At that point the sticky note gets lifted off, and I ask them more questions: "Did you feel shame when you felt put down? When you blamed your wife? When you pulled away from her?" Usually, clients respond with great surprise and relief that the missing piece has been found. At that point, I might discuss the elephant in the room through humor, stories, or examples of how it's a common experience to react this way to painful experiences. This normalizes their shame and allows them to begin talking about it and begin the process of healing their shame.

Once you understand what shame is and can identify and acknowledge when you are feeling shame, the journey begins. When you can withdraw from a situation even a little bit and reassess it, noting the way shame plays out in your feelings and behavior, you are on the road to change. Shame is a primary emotion with a useful purpose; trying to eliminate shame is a fool's errand. However, shame can be transformed into something positive, and this book is meant to help you transform your toxic, defeating, and destructive shame into healthy shame.

## PRACTICES

### Working with the Reactions to Shame

First, take a few minutes to reflect on this chapter, which may have brought up some difficult feelings for you. Notice if there's a part of you that can take in the success of reading this material. Next, try out the following breathing practice: inhaling a sense of peace for the count of nine and then breathing out stress and shame for a count of ten. Do that repeatedly for a couple of minutes—breathe in peace, exhale shame. Finally, just sit silently and notice what your thoughts and feelings are. Remind yourself that all of you is welcome here.

The next part of this practice involves reviewing the reactions discussed above and journaling. Be gentle with yourself as you continue. Know that it can be triggering to review this material, and it can be easy to put yourself down for having these reactions. Consider that these reactions to shame are something that happens in our nervous system and that we don't really have much control once it gets started. If you notice that part of you is putting yourself down as you do this exercise, tell yourself that you're engaging in important research. The research is personal, very personal. No one else can do it for you.

Notice which of the reactions to shame is your first response. Go to the relevant section below (that is, Attack Self, Attack Other, and so on) and gently engage with the recommended practice. Remember that this exercise is mostly about learning more about yourself and accepting the ways you react to shame. Knowing more about your reactions can be helpful, but only if you don't get too triggered. If that happens, please return to the beginning of this practice or go back to a practice that worked for you earlier in the book.

## Attack Self

Think of some of the ways your inner critic puts you down. In what ways does perfectionism play out in your life? What messages do you hear that tell you it's all your fault? Pause here to consider all the ways you react to shame by attacking yourself. Thank yourself with great kindness as you write down some of the lines the Attack Self tends to say. Following the example below, write the sentence or phrase, and remember to thank yourself at the end for your good work.

### Attack-Self Responses

> *It's my fault.*
>
> *I never get it right.*
>
> *I can't get anything right.*

## Attack Other

Maybe your first reaction to shame is to Attack Others or put them down. Do you pass the hot potato out of anger? What are some of the ways you have contempt for others? Do you absolutely hate it when you are criticized by others or not respected? How often do you feel it's the other person's fault? Pause and write about this for a while. Again, we're simply doing a little personal research here. There's no need to believe or argue with these messages; you're just noticing. Write down the Attack-Other messages you most often hear or say and then remember to thank yourself after each.

### Attack-Other Responses

> *It's all their fault.*
>
> *Why can't they get it right?*

*They're so stupid!*

*I can't count on them because . . .*

Please keep in mind that these are responses to explore, not actions to express. As elsewhere, observe them quietly and with kindness.

## Deny

Consider when you tend to go numb or blank. After something difficult happens, do you regularly comment that it wasn't so bad? What addictions have you had in your life? Do you get lost in drugs or sex or alcohol? Fill in the following list mindfully and return to the opening of this practice if you need to.

### Deny Responses

*I dissociate or lose track when . . .*

*I get numb or blank when . . .*

*Some of my addictions are . . .*

*Other addictions include . . .*

*I say "It didn't really happen" about . . .*

*I say "It wasn't so bad" about . . .*

## Fawn/Cling

It is common for women to be put in a Fawn/Cling position in their families and in a largely patriarchal society. Of course, men can also experience a Fawn/Cling reaction to shame. This response to shame can be shocking or embarrassing to the person experiencing it. When do you have the Fawn reaction to shame? This could take the form of pausing or going silent around others, just like a fawn. You might be waiting and watching but not saying anything—hiding in plain sight. When do you Cling to others, even when you know it's not in your best interests? How often are unable to access your anger?

## Fawn Responses

> *I fawn when . . .*
>
> *I usually hide when . . .*
>
> *I'm scared because . . .*

## Cling Responses

> *I may cling and bond with someone without realizing it when . . .*
>
> *My anger remains frozen when . . .*

## Withdraw

Notice what Withdraw reactions happen for you. When do you pull in or look away? Is there a sense you need to retreat in order to lick your wounds? Again, we're exercising kind curiosity here. Do you find yourself isolating, feeling mistrust, or sometimes losing faith and hope? How often do you feel depressed? It's important to let yourself do the research here and notice your reactions without getting fully into them. If you get too triggered, go back to the meditative opening to this practice. If not, please fill in the following in your journal:

## Withdraw Responses

> *I withdraw and pull in when . . .*
>
> *I lick my wounds when . . .*
>
> *I reassess when . . .*
>
> *I isolate when . . .*

*I mistrust when . . .*

*I lose faith and hope when . . .*

*I get depressed when . . .*

Give yourself a big hug for filling out these explorations. Stand up and shake it out. Wiggle your hands, stomp your feet, and let it go if you can. And if you can't, you can imagine moving your hands and giving yourself a hug. Learning more about your reactions to shame might be challenging or triggering, but it can help you understand yourself and the people near you a little better. In the end, it will feel as if a huge weight has been lifted from your chest. Put that weight down for a while and celebrate the work you've already done.

4

# Healthy Shame

*Healthy shame is an emotion which signals us about our limits. Like all emotions, healthy shame is an energy-in-motion. Like all emotions it moves us to get our basic needs met.*

—John Bradshaw

*You can't let your failures define you. You have to let your failures teach you. You have to let them show you what to do differently the next time.*

—Barack Obama

The idea of healthy shame is perhaps the most transformative, mind-bending, life-changing concept we teach. It goes against all the conventional wisdom about shame. Most people think shame is unilaterally dangerous and destructive and that we need to transcend it or eliminate it from our lives. The problem is that shame is an essential primary emotion—everyone has it in some form, and it's not going away. Shame is wired into our nervous system for a reason. We couldn't get rid of it if we tried any more than we could eliminate anger, fear, or grief.

The concept of healthy shame isn't ours alone. There's a small but determined minority of us trying to get this concept of healthy shame out there, including our friend John Amodeo, who uses the term *friendly shame.*[1]

> The destructive, life-stopping force we know as shame can be transformed into something healthy and useful.

A certain kind of shame is useful for anybody who wants to have productive relationships with other people. Shame helps us recognize that we aren't alone in the world, that we need to obey certain rules and guidelines in order to be part of society, and that we need to acknowledge and be concerned about how other people feel. This is what we're referring to as *healthy shame*, which is quite different from *toxic shame.* Healthy shame leads to more rewarding relationships with ourselves and others. If enough people acquired it, healthy shame would lead to a happier, healthier society and a better world. This is the good news: the destructive, life-stopping force we know as shame can be transformed into something healthy and useful.

In toxic shame, the nervous system freezes. We lose track of what's happening around us, and we can only focus on our flaws and lacks. In contrast, healthy shame invites us to pause, pay attention, and reassess ourselves and our environment. This is how healthy shame helps us learn and understand how to function successfully and joyfully within the limits of restrictions put on us by both nature and society. As humans, we have limited abilities and control. We're imperfect; we make mistakes. Shame helps us fulfill our survival need for connection and for being part of something larger than ourselves by helping us observe norms and behaviors. Shame mostly becomes problematic when we neglect or penalize the occurrence of basic human feelings, needs, and drives.

## A Therapist's Thoughts on Healthy Shame

I want to thank Bret and Sheila for helping me learn that shame isn't something to get rid of. At first, I thought that counter-shaming techniques should be about eradicating shame or at least canceling it out somehow. Now I see that counter-shaming is more about transformation, about working with toxic shame in such a way that enhances our overall experience of all it means to be human.

Healthy shame is a goal, a process. We begin by creating enough space so we can access healthy shame because we can't do a whole lot except focus on survival when our nervous system gets highjacked. But when we gain some distance from our shame, pendulate to resources, and open up our breathing, we can begin to see our situation differently. As we stated in the last chapter, withdrawing can be a beneficial reaction at times—when shame is an eruption from our past, we can step away, calm ourselves, and return to the present moment. Once we gain space from the shaming incident, we can reassess and bring our strengths online instead of just trying to forget all about it, move past it, or attack ourselves and other people.

Most people know that being kind to yourself feels a lot better than shaming, but simply loving yourself as you are isn't enough to heal the terrible feelings and self-talk involved in shame. However, if we unravel some of the shame, recognize where we have broken intrapersonal bridges, work to repair them, and accept our imperfections and limitations, we can finally begin to transform our shame. Without this multidimensional work, we'll continue to remain stuck in unconscious cycles of trying to feed, exercise, drink, or self-abuse our shame away. We must discover and truly feel what has been bound with, concealed by, and distorted by our shame. While there's much we can do on our own, it can go a long way to get help from a friend, caring relative, teacher, or helping professional who is compassionate, accepting, and knowledgeable about shame and how it works.

*A Student's Reflection*

As I go about my life, I can practice noticing how I am responding and reacting to shame. Shame is everywhere, and it so easily pops up in any situation or interaction. It's easy to be taken over by a reaction to negative shame without even noticing it. How aware I am about what unhealthy shame feels like, how it tends to show up for me, and how I react to it seems to directly relate to my own ability to interrupt the habitual pattern of a particular shame response and support myself in the process of moving into a healthy shame response.

This chapter includes several active ways that we encourage healthy shame in ourselves, our clients, and our students.

## ENCOURAGE COMPASSIONATE CURIOSITY

As we mentioned at the end of chapter 2, curiosity operates as an antidote to shame. We're not talking about cold, scientific curiosity here, but a gentle and kind curiosity that's detached enough to allow us to be with our feelings without becoming lost in them. Eugene Gendlin's *focusing* practice is a useful way to develop compassionate curiosity about ourselves. Gendlin employed the concept of the *felt sense* (which can be made up of a combination of physical sensations, emotions, images, and thoughts) to explore what's happening with us and gain clarity about our *unclear edges*. Focusing is typically done in partnership, and Gendlin and his students (like Ann Weiser Cornell, who we trained under) have created a structure to the practice so people who are not trained therapists or helpers can help each other.[2]

## GET MOVING

Shame keeps us stuck. It's like a whirlpool, drawing us deeper and deeper into it. Like the mythical Sirens' song, it grabs our attention and keeps us from seeing what's going on around us, making it difficult to focus on anything else. For that reason, sometimes it's helpful to shake things up, break out of the shame posture, and activate our body by stomping, laughing, going out for a walk, dancing, or hugging yourself.

### Shame Is Everywhere

One of Bret's clients had been a talented hockey player in high school. Gary had even been up for an athletic scholarship, but then he became depressed and stopped playing altogether. Bret's first piece of advice to him was that he join a local amateur hockey team. Gary thought about it, and at the beginning of our next session, he announced, "I'm doing it. I'm going back to play hockey again. I love it, I need it, and I'm ready to face the challenges ahead." Sure enough, almost as soon as Gary got himself back on the ice, his depression started to lift. (As mentioned in chapter 2, we believe it's an anger-grief-fear-shame bind that results in depression.)

Movement doesn't have to be athletic, sports-oriented, or even physical. It also helps to engage in learning-focused activities or artistic pursuits, like visual art and music (and there's nothing quite like singing to open your breathing). As Martin Luther King Jr. said, "If you can't fly, run. If you can't run, walk. If you can't walk, crawl. But by all means, keep moving."

## MARSHAL YOUR RESOURCES

After we gain some space from a shaming situation and start to shift our focus, we need to remember our resources. Shame freezes our access to our memories, mental clarity and perspective, and even some physical movements. Our brain tends to go over the shaming incident repeatedly and, in the bargain, brings up other shame-related events from the past. It forgets or bypasses all the people, animals, and places that once supported us or that could be doing so in the present. Ideally, when we experience shame, we learn how to pendulate to our resources.

We don't typically think of breathing as one of our primary resources because it's so omnipresent and usually unconscious, but consider where we'd be without it. We could go without sex for a lifetime (as unpleasant as that might be), we could live without food for weeks, and we could go without water for days, but we wouldn't last more than a few minutes without air. When we're in the shame posture, our head drops forward and our chest collapses in on itself, constraining our breathing. While breathing is involuntary, we can control and change the pattern. The part of the breath we have the most control over is the exhalation. The more we exhale, the more breath enters our body on the inhale. There are a number of ways to alter our breathing (sighing, screaming, yawning) and thereby modify our nervous system, mood, and thoughts.

Breathing can help us access our imagination and helpful memories. For example, remembering the people and animals who have cared about us can help us feel safe and joyful. We can also call to mind real or imaginary people (say, from literature or movies) who inspire us or model some resourceful behavior. Recalling times when we accomplished something challenging can remind us that we are strong and capable. All of these practices shift our focus away from the shaming situation and empower us to view the bigger picture. The shame might be quite difficult to deal with, but we also have resources than can see us through to the other side.

## A Student's List of Resources

We often ask our students to write a list of their resources, internal and external. For inspiration in coming up with a list of your own, here's an abbreviated version of what one of our students wrote:

- My athleticism and how I can tap into my inner warrior when I participate in endurance sports.

- My ability to connect with animals, plants, and humans deeply and with intense openness and compassion.

- My connection to nature, especially redwood trees. It helps me tap into awe and gratitude, and it is my conduit to spirituality.

- My meditation and gratitude practices, and my ability to use my breath to ground and calm myself in the moment.

- My art practice that allows my emotions and experience to be expressed in profound ways that words could never capture.

- My pets. How my cat purrs and likes to hold my hand. My dog's kisses, companionship, and ability to make me laugh.

- The crystals, jewelry, sparkles, and rainbows that excite my inner child and make me happy.

- The joy I derive from cooking food from the farm I belong to and the deliciousness of seasonal, fresh food.

- Being able to ask for support despite it being scary or overwhelming.

Other people can be excellent resources when we're in shame. Just being with people we trust can help us stop spinning out about what happened to us and all the stuff we're telling ourselves is wrong with us. Sometimes, as our student noted in their list, animals can be a tremendous resource. They might not be able to reply when we talk about our felt sense, but they simply love us and help us calm down.

## Michelle Obama and Her Aunt

In *Becoming*, Michelle Obama tells the story of growing up on the South Side of Chicago.[3] She talks about learning piano from her aunt, who was a music teacher. Michelle always wanted to play faster because she wanted to go on to whatever was next, but her aunt kept slowing her down. On her aunt's piano, Michelle could find middle C easily because of the slight discoloration of that particular key from all the years of students playing it.

At her first recital, Michelle walked up to the stage and immediately noticed that all the keys on the concert piano were polished and shiny white. Without the off-white middle C, Michelle went blank. She couldn't figure out where to put her hands. She couldn't even remember the piece that she had practiced for so long. Michelle simply stood there frozen, looking helplessly at the shiny keys.

For her, the pause seemed to last forever. Then her aunt quietly walked on stage, stood next to Michelle, and put the tip of her finger where middle C was. Suddenly, Michelle could remember the song, and she played it as well as she usually did. This moment of calm, compassionate, and precise support was all that Michelle needed in the moment. ☀

## TALK TO THE INNER CRITIC

We mentioned the inner critic in the Attack-Self portion of chapter 3. This is the cognitive part of shame, that voice inside of us that criticizes us, tells us we can't do anything right, and tries to convince us we're not worthy. The inner critic is constantly talking. Sometimes we can hear it; other times it just runs in the background. All kinds of things can activate it—we do something we don't feel good about, we feel dismissed or the butt of a joke, or maybe we feel misunderstood, ignored, or unseen.

We need to develop a counter-shaming voice in order to move toward healthy shame. To begin with, remember the quote from the last chapter: "The perfect is the enemy of the good." This is an important concept to understand when dealing with shame because quite a bit of our shame comes from the impossible expectations placed upon us by society, our families, and in turn, ourselves. Our drive for perfection can keep us from appreciating what we do well and all the things we have going for us. And the shame voice is an expert at telling us that we're no good, that something is bad, wrong, or flawed about us.

Here's an example of how counter-shaming works. When we notice the inner critic jabbering away at us, we simply reply back with something along these lines: *You're right; I'm not perfect. Nobody's perfect. I made a mistake, but that's normal. I can learn from my mistakes and strive to be good enough, because I'll never be perfect.*

Over time, we can learn to develop and instill a kind voice that talks back to the inner critic or at least tells the younger parts of us not to be fooled by the shame voice. Sure, we mess up sometimes, but that's part of life. What matters is that we're kind to ourselves and others and do our best. That's the sort of voice, too, that we want to hear from the people close to us. They may say things like, "You're going to get through this," or "Yeah, you made a mistake, but it's not the end of the world," thereby reminding us of the bigger picture we can't always see in the moment by ourselves. If they share messages like this with compassion, it counters the harsher shaming voice inside us.

Below are two useful language changes—*both-and* and using the language of *parts*—you can employ when talking to your inner critic and counter-shaming yourself.

> Every strength is a weakness, and
> every weakness is a strength.

## BOTH-AND

Much of Western culture relies on binary, either-or thinking. Things can either be one way (for example, *good*) or another (*bad*). We can see this as far back as Aristotle's *law of the excluded middle*, in which contradicting ideas can't have an intermediary. Surprisingly, this is not a universal concept, and modern physics has called the scientific basis of such into question (for example, light is said to be *both* particle *and* wave). Intuitively, most of us know that we don't need to exclude one truth because something different also happens to be true. Using *both-and* language acknowledges this as an antidote to either-or thinking, which can also help us foster healthy shame.

The shame voice is known for being rigid. It only presents one side of a much larger picture, and that side isn't too flattering—it's mostly weaknesses and flaws. But we can have a conversation with the inner critic that goes something like, *You're right. I do have weaknesses and flaws. And I also have strengths and gifts.* Notice how *and* started that last sentence. Using *and* instead of *but* acknowledges that both are true—strengths and weaknesses coexist.

And if you really want to shake things up with your shaming voice, remind it that every strength is a weakness and every weakness is a strength. It all depends on context. A strength, like discipline or work drive, is wonderful within measure, but taken too far can easily cross over into something harmful. You might get a lot done, but can you relax and enjoy it? We generally think that strengths are preferable and that limitations are detrimental, but the opposite can just as easily be true.

> The shame voice—the inner critic, the internal shamer—is just one of our parts.

## USE PARTS LANGUAGE

In English, the word *I* is somewhat fixed and permanent. "I am going to the store," "I am studying math," "I have seven dollars on me," "I used to work at a car wash"—sentences like these are useful shorthand, but using *I* in this way often doesn't fit or feel right when trying to describe our inner experience. We might say, "I'm angry," but the truth is we may be feeling several different emotions at the same time, especially when shame is involved. It might sound normal (and quite sad) to hear someone say, "I hate myself," but it's also imprecise. Who hates who? Who is criticizing who? Is the *I* one thing and the *myself* another?

It's far more accurate to speak of ourselves as a collection of parts. Inner Relationship Focusing, Internal Family Systems, and other therapeutic and self-help forms use this sort of language to help us understand what's going on inside us better. "Part of me is really angry at my inner child" might sound long-winded, but it illustrates a degree of self-understanding that can help us with shame. Inner battles between different aspects of ourselves are often our most confusing and painful struggles.

The shame voice—the inner critic, the internal shamer—is just one of our parts. We acknowledge as much when we talk back to it. When we don't have those conversations and let the shame voice run the show, we become entirely identified with that particular part of us. And so it takes over. Talking back to it breaks the pattern of identification and reminds the shamer that it's merely one part among many.

## QUALITIES OF HEALTHY SHAME

When we connect to our resources, pendulate, and counter-shame our inner critic with any of the techniques above, we begin to bring our healthy shame qualities online. We may not be able to connect with all the qualities covered next (and some will no doubt come easier than others), but even one of them is often enough to change everything the next time you feel shame.

### Self-Compassion

Having self-compassion is the missing piece for somebody with a voracious inner critic. It's also one of the most difficult elements of healthy shame. In some ways, self-compassion is the gatekeeper to healthy shame.

#### Sheila and Self-Compassion

When I was younger, I could feel self-compassion when I was meditating or moving or dancing alone. In those moments, the shame I carried and the ways in which I put myself down would disappear for a time. I could be still and put my hand on my heart and remember the kind words of friends, teachers, and more than one of my therapists, and that would calm the break inside of me. I would find a way to witness myself with kindness and their words. This is something I try to offer my students and clients too. When they can contact self-compassion, even for a few minutes, they can restore the inner bridge that their shame has broken. Maybe they can even hear my voice reminding them that they're okay or remember me saying, "It's going to be okay." And then maybe they can connect with themselves and the world more, feeling more whole and loving.

It's always helpful to visit or remember someone who's been kind and compassionate to us. We can also create a mental image of someone like this—or bring to mind someone in history (like Mother Teresa or Thich Nhat Hanh or Martin Luther King Jr.) known for their incredible compassion—and imagine that they're showering us with their brilliant kindness.

## Taking Responsibility

Until we know and acknowledge our own responsibility in a situation in which we were shamed, it's hard for us to release the toxic shame and move into healthy shame. Unfortunately, the shame voice tends to either take *all* the responsibility (Attack Self) or place the blame solely on others (Attack Others). Healthy shame means that we know the truth of *both-and* and recognize the subtleties involve in the bigger picture.

### Laurie's Shame

Laurie was a middle-aged client who was still carrying heavy childhood shame. When she was five years old, her mother often went out and left Laurie in charge of her two-year-old brother. One time, her little brother peed on the couch, and when their mother came home, she was livid. She berated Laurie and called her names. The shaming stuck. So, many years later, Laurie hung her head and teared up in a session when she thought about that shaming event. "I was bad," she cried, "I didn't do my job." We had to remind her that it shouldn't have been her job to supervise her brother in the first place. In fact, it was her mother's job to supervise both of them or to get another adult to be in charge when she had to go out. It's wrong to leave a five-year-old to supervise a two-year-old, for obvious reasons, and a soiled couch is certainly not the worst thing that could have happened. Instead of Laurie's mother taking responsibility and expressing healthy shame about what happened when she was out (thereby learning a lesson and changing her behavior in the future), she launched into Attack-Other behavior and dumped her toxic shame on Laurie, who still carried it decades later. But it was never Laurie's shame to carry in the first place; it was her mother's.

## A Client Takes Responsibility

Another client of ours had a daughter who was doing drugs. They'd been alienated for some time, and our client was attacking herself for what had happened. It was important for her to learn to acknowledge that she *did* have some responsibility to bear while also reminding her that she'd raised her kids all by herself with ample childhood shame of her own. She hadn't been a perfect mother, *and* she'd done the best she could, considering. Additionally, there wasn't much she could currently do to prevent her daughter from using drugs. But our client could take responsibility, forgive herself, and love her daughter the best she could.

## Humility

Humility is another crucial aspect of healthy shame. None of us is perfect. Everybody has strengths and weaknesses; everybody has limitations. That's essentially what it means to be human. Recognizing this keeps us humble, especially when our limitations and challenges begin to add up as we age.

## Bret's Experience with Humility

In our workshops, I always illustrate healthy humility by saying, "I really wish I could fly." That may sound silly, but when most of us are kids, we really want to be able to fly, and even as adults, we sometimes have flying dreams. But the fact that we know we can't fly keeps us from jumping off tall buildings and flapping our arms—which would lead to unfavorable results. While it may not be too difficult to accept that I can't fly, these days there are things that I could do when I was younger that I just can't do anymore. Sometimes that upsets me. But if I spent all my time worrying about it, I'd just go into shame. And if I let shame drive me to do things that I'm no longer physically equipped to do, I'm just going to wind up with more shame because I'm probably going to hurt myself. With age comes certain weaknesses, and accepting this is a way to connect to my own humility. Age also comes with new strengths. It's important for me to accept that both are true.

## Bill's Journey

Bill, a client of Bret's in his sixties, had once been a superior athlete. It was hard for him to come to terms with not being as physically capable as he once had been. That meant he would go out and overexert himself considerably and end up straining and hurting himself, and then he would be laid up for a couple of days or a week and, as a result, go into tremendous shame. It took time to help him accept and come to terms with the fact that he'd become older and he just couldn't do all that he'd been able to do before. This client had also been a teacher, and he loved to learn. It turned out that he'd been wanting to learn Mandarin but hadn't done much about it. Bret suggested going online and finding people that he could learn from. He found a website that connected him to English speakers in China who wanted to improve their English, and Bill ended up spending many happy hours trading sessions with five or six learning partners. In the process, he developed a circle of new friends. So, even if he'd become more limited physically, Bill was more than able to foster other interests and share his gifts.

## Seeing the Big Picture

Toxic shame narrows our perspective and gives us tunnel vision. In healthy shame, we're able to look at the big picture—past events, present circumstances, future considerations, and all the people who might be involved.

There's a story we once heard about a ruler who assembled a group of wise elders and asked them to come up with a statement that would always be true. The elders secluded themselves for six months and discussed the matter at length until they finally came to an agreement. The statement they agreed on was *This, too, shall pass.* As elders ourselves, we can confirm that the journey of life entails countless ups and downs. What happened to you in childhood, or whatever you're telling yourself you did wrong, doesn't have to stick with you forever.

## Precision

Shame fogs our thinking and makes us confused. When we work with clients, we always ask a lot of questions in order to clarify the blurry narratives of shame. This can start to open up the reality of what happened as seen through a client's current perception, instead of the limited view they experienced as a child. We begin to see the finer points and details more clearly.

An example of the power of precision is when a person says, "I can't go back to see my family for the holidays—every single one of them is against me." Usually, it turns out with deeper probing that in a family that's been grouped into "everyone" versus "no one" (the client), there's usually at least one relative—often an uncle, aunt, or cousin—who is on their side. This person just got lost in the story of "everyone." When shame's in charge, things blend together, so it's important to dial in and gain clarity to see the bigger picture.

## Humor

Humor lightens the situation and produces a pendulation—it takes you out of where you're stuck and brings a certain level of lightness, a certain level of distraction, which is important when dealing with shame. While all humor can provide valuable distraction and pendulation, we're talking about warm-hearted humor, the kind that doesn't shame others and that encourages us to not take ourselves or our problems too seriously. "Angels can fly because they can take themselves lightly" is a saying we're very fond of.

One of the first things that dictators try to do when they seize power is get rid of the comedians. Humor challenges the status quo; laughter shifts and frees energy. It's hard to be contracted and stuck when we're laughing. Humor breaks through shame and provides new perspectives.

## Vulnerability

When the interpersonal bridge gets broken too often and we experience toxic shame, another bridge gets broken—the *intra*personal bridge. We have a core need to be fully ourselves, and we also have a core need to connect with others and be seen, accepted, and loved. Ideally, these two needs go hand in hand, but shame places them at odds with each other. We feel forced to choose between them.

### A Teacher Copes with Difference

Everywhere I look, there are reminders of the shame of imperfection. It took a long time for me to feel comfortable with losing my hearing, but once I could no longer escape acknowledging that I could hear very little and began admitting it to colleagues, I became brave enough eventually to share my diagnosis with my students. It opened a door I had not anticipated as we bonded over shared experiences. I was struggling like them in a world that was moving too fast for me to process in normal ways. I needed accommodations too. My new disability—even more so my *admitted disability*—helped my students normalize their experiences. We gained a new mutual understanding. We spoke the same language in a way we never had before because now the conversation came from experience and from the heart. Coming face-to-face with the societal stigmas associated with *special needs* and *needing accommodations* gave me the gift of insight that enriched my work. My students and I were all different together. And I was their advocate. 🌅

Brené Brown says that vulnerability is the opposite of shame.[4] Shame thrives on secrecy, and the action tendency of shame is to protect ourselves by hiding and disappearing. Vulnerability, on the other hand, involves making the decision to reach out to others and reveal ourselves.

## Discernment

It's unwise and potentially dangerous to be vulnerable without discernment. While precision has a strong cognitive component and helps us see things clearly, discernment comes more from the gut or intuition and is what helps us make choices based on that clarity. When we are ready to reveal ourselves to others, we need to know which people are suitable recipients and how much it's okay to share with them. Is the person safe to tell our story to? When's the right time to share? How much should we hold back?

If we grow up with toxic shame, we can be drawn toward people who shame us. The discernment of healthy shame keeps us from constantly returning to poisoned water. Healthy shame helps us set boundaries, determine what we will accept and what we won't put up with. Discernment teaches us that words and actions that harm ourselves and others are no longer acceptable.

Discernment helps us to not just go along with what someone else asks of us or wants us to do. It allows us to ask questions. It gives us a sense of whether situations and people are right for us. Very often, discernment starts with a feeling that something is wrong—a feeling we typically experience in our gut. Toxic shame can cause us to override that feeling and put us in peril. We don't always have to act on that feeling, but we do have to explore why we have it. For example, if we can't get straight answers to the questions we ask ourselves and others, it could mean that we're in danger.

Healthy shame teaches us that we have to make choices in life, that one choice may preclude another, that our time and energy are limited, and that we can't have or accomplish everything. The path we choose to follow may eliminate a different and potentially favorable path or, at the least, make that path difficult to try out later. As we get older, some paths we could have followed become closed to us. The discernment of healthy shame helps us accept where we are right now, which in turn empowers us on the journey we have taken.

It's healthy shame's job to teach us important lessons and help us grow. To that end, it can sometimes make us uncomfortable so that we become more aware and resourceful. A long time ago, every kid wanted to get their hands on a box of Cracker Jacks, which had developed an amazing marketing strategy. Cracker Jacks were basically a box of crunchy sugary stuff that in truth didn't taste that good, but every box came with a little toy or prize in it. There were three approaches to Cracker Jacks: eat the snack slowly and wait to get to the prize at the bottom, gobble it up to find the toy faster, or just empty the box of all that crunchy stuff and grab the prize. Whichever way we went about it, we only purchased Cracker Jacks because of the promised treasure in every box. The discernment of healthy shame is the prize we get from the shaming experience.

### Getting to Healthy Shame

I felt a lot of shame about something that happened last week. I spent quite a bit of energy this week in the reactions of unhealthy shame, mostly being angry and defensive and spinning the situation in my head over and over again. I'm wondering how much of my response to the situation I could have shifted by stepping back for a moment, looking at the bigger picture, staying humble, being vulnerable, extending compassion to myself, and *then* reengaging with others.

## HEALTHY SHAME AND A BASKETBALL SUPERSTAR

Stephen Curry isn't physically imposing. Six-foot-two is above normal height, but Curry is often the shortest man on a basketball court, and his thin build makes him look even smaller. Even so, Curry is widely considered among the best in the game, and his unique skill set has inspired average-sized athletes all over the world to feel that they, too, have a shot at playing professional sports.

All of this happened due to Curry's healthy shame response to his limitations. As a child, Curry wanted to play professional basketball (as his father, Dell, had done in the 1980s and 1990s), but he was often discouraged because of his smaller weight and height. His father told the young Curry that he had to become outstanding at shooting baskets, otherwise no coach would even give him a second look. And that's exactly what he did. Curry could have given up on his dream and allowed himself to freeze in despair, but he never stopped trying to improve his skills on the court. His story is just one notable example of what healthy shame can look like.

### Bret Loses It (Then Recovers)

Yesterday, I discovered that all the additions and changes I made to this chapter, which I was very proud of and which took me all day to write, had disappeared from my Word document. To put it mildly, I was not pleased. I spent several hours trying to get that work back, frantically reviewing endless Google instructions, but nothing worked. Because I tend toward the Attack-Other shame reaction, I had some choice words for Microsoft for not creating an automatic backup that actually worked. And then I also did a little bit of the Attack-Self reaction by blaming myself for not mastering Word before starting this project and for not being able to follow Google's instructions.

As a result, I stayed up until 3:00 am and blew my diet, trying in vain to calm down and comfort myself. My shame reaction to being neglected by well-meaning but absent parents as a kid was to develop a strong belief that I have to do everything by myself and that no one is competent enough or willing to help me. But another part of me was saying that the material could be recovered, that I just had to find people who had the competence and willingness to help. This voice gained the upper hand for a minute, but then the shame voice took over again, and all I could do was watch myself go through this internal mini drama. Eventually, I was able to remind myself that *this, too, shall pass.* Either someone would help me get the material back or I would simply rewrite it. It wasn't the end of the world.

Early the next morning, I called my computer store and was told that they couldn't help me over the phone; I'd have to close down the computer and bring it in, and maybe, just maybe—after hours of scanning the memory—they *might* be able to find the material I was missing. Rather than lose the computer for days for what was likely a failed mission, I chose to take the day to rewrite all the changes. I felt a surge of energy and calm when I made the decision. I was going to do it myself. I would learn from my mistake and press the save button every couple of minutes and be sure to never lose so much material ever again. I figured I could remember most of what I had done the day before and that it would probably only take me three hours instead of the six I had originally spent writing and editing before, but as soon as I started, I felt a deep pit open in my stomach. I couldn't remember anything.

I sat at the computer all day. Eventually, I opened my door and emerged from my room, having made all the additions and brought the manuscript back to where it had been before all the losses. I felt a huge surge of pride. I had done it! I was back on track. Except for my eyes hurting from the strain of working on the computer nonstop and my shoulder hurting from pressing the save key over and over obsessively, I felt great. My weaknesses—a tendency to obsess over mistakes and try to fix them immediately, as well as a belief that I have to do everything myself—had, in this case, served as strengths. Once I'd finished, I was ready to reemerge and join the world again. ☀

## FROM TOXIC SHAME TO HEALTHY SHAME
## IN DISNEY'S *FROZEN*

In the beloved movie *Frozen*, Elsa, the princess-heroine, possesses a great and dangerous power that makes her different from everyone else: she can freeze water at will. As a child, Elsa wasn't yet in control of her abilities, and she inadvertently injured her younger sister, which resulted in Elsa feeling tremendous shame. The power scared her parents, who told Elsa to keep it hidden, so Elsa locks herself away from everyone, including Anna, her younger sister. Things go from bad to worse when their parents die, leaving them orphans.

When Elsa's power is discovered, she abandons the city and castle of her childhood to live alone in the snowy mountains nearby. But her freedom to be herself and use her power however she wants comes at a great cost—in withdrawing, Elsa's abilities wreak havoc on her homeland and Anna.

Elsa's sister, Anna, has her own shame journey, having experienced abandonment first from her sister and then from her parents. Abandonment and neglect are as powerful as more direct acts of shaming and abuse when it comes to producing shame. But Anna never internalizes the shame. She maintains total innocence and a childlike sense of power in spite of her situation, and so she falls in love with the first man she meets. Anna has developed a lack of healthy shame, which leaves her naive and unaware of human limitations. If toxic shame is a state of freeze, shown so clearly in Elsa, then healthy shame is a cautionary pause, a quality of checking things out, knowing to look before you leap. Anna can't see difficulties and danger when they are clearly right before her, so she's taken in by Hans, a sociopathic social climber. Anna's rushing into dangerous situations leads to her being inadvertently wounded by Elsa's magical power to create cold. She is in danger of turning to ice and freezing to death.

> Healthy shame reminds us all that we have
> something special to bring to the world.

Eventually, the self-sacrificing love of her sister calls Elsa back to the city, heals her of her toxic shame, and teaches her to embrace her difference and control her power. She heals her sister, and Elsa learns to take her special place in the city, where she can be appreciated for her gifts and who she truly is. Once Elsa learns to control her power, her difference becomes a beautiful and valuable strength—a gift that delights and benefits the entire city.

## SHARING YOUR GIFT

One of the wonderful fruits of healthy shame is being able to share your gifts with the world. Just as Elsa became a benevolent ruler of her kingdom, beautifying the landscape with her power, we all have something to offer once we transform our toxic shame. It's toxic shame that tries to convince us we don't have a gift to share. Healthy shame reminds us all that we have something special to bring to the world, especially to the people and animals who are most dear to us.

Contacting and expressing our gifts brings meaning and purpose to our lives. As we emerge from toxic shame, our gift becomes clear. Either we figure out a way to offer it to others or we find out that we've already been sharing it. As Albert Einstein put it:

> Strange is our situation here upon earth. Each of us comes for a short visit, not knowing why, yet sometimes seeming to divine a purpose. From the standpoint of daily life, however, there is one thing we do know: that man is here for the sake of other men—above all for those upon whose smile and well-being our own happiness depends, and also for the countless unknown souls with whose fate we are connected by a bond of sympathy. Many times a day I realize how much my own outer and inner

life is built upon the labors of my fellow men, both living and dead, and how earnestly I must exert myself in order to give in return as much as I have received.[5]

## PRACTICES

## Healthy Shame Visualization

Breathe in and out at your own pace. After a few minutes of settling into this practice, let yourself call to mind something you feel embarrassed about, something you feel self-conscious about, something that maybe your inner critic has been bringing up lately. Is there a part of you that's been feeling embarrassed, rejected, or put down?

With this feeling or memory in mind, imagine that you're going on a walk. Let's say you're walking down a hill, one step after another, and eventually you approach the shore of a wide river. You see a boat there waiting for you. It's the healthy shame boat. As you step into the boat, your body sways a little this way and that way, and you feel all of those movements with compassion as you slowly situate yourself in the boat. Remember that if you stand back up, the boat is going to rock back and forth, so find a place in the boat where you can sit down with your solid center underneath you.

When you're ready, gently push or release the boat into the river. Allow self-compassion to float over you and ask yourself if you have any responsibility for the shame event that set you on this journey. Breathing in and out, notice your part in whatever happened—something you did or didn't do. Just pay attention to any part that might be yours. If you find anything, hold it gently in your hands or place it in your chest with kindness. Then take whatever isn't yours and just release it downstream in the river.

Breathe in and out at your own pace and let yourself feel whatever's going on in this moment. Look out upon the shore on both sides of the boat as you float along. Feel what it's like—the humility of being human. Maybe you blew it; maybe something happened that you didn't know about and wish you had. Whatever it was, just feel the humility of your current experience and notice if there's anything from it that you want to keep with you in the boat. Is there something that you want to explore further? If not, release even more of it into the water.

Now, as you continue to float in your healthy shame boat, let your sense of humor come to the surface. Maybe there's a favorite joke you like to tell, or you can bring to mind one of your funny friends. One of my favorite jokes is about a club where they don't even tell the jokes anymore. Because they've all been doing it together for so long, they just shout out the numbers of the jokes. Somebody says, "47," and everybody laughs. Somebody else says, "26," and everybody cracks up again. For some reason, that joke makes me laugh or smile without fail. Try it out for yourself. What are some things that connect you to your sense of humor?

Now it's time to notice the big picture. As you breathe in and out, look around you at the water, the sky, the riverbanks, the trees, and so on. Maybe your river is the mighty Colorado, and on either side of you are these amazing rocks and majestic cliffs of the Grand Canyon. Think of the fact that you're alive in this incredibly original moment in time in all of humanity, and there's an opportunity here to change the tide of shame. Take a mental snapshot of your big picture, put it in your pocket or maybe keep it safe in your camera, and just notice as many details as you can as you continue to float down the river. Keep breathing at your own pace and enjoy this precious time you're having with yourself.

Now imagine whether you're alone in the boat or there are other people with you. Who else is in the boat? Continue to breathe in and out and think about any reassessment you'd like to have around this shame experience before you go back to your life on the shore. What would it be? Know that in a moment you'll be headed back, that you're going to be getting out of the boat and reengaging the world. But after you get back on shore, anytime you want to, you can come back to this moment and replay this whole thing again. You could replay it in your own mind, in your own voice—all these components of healthy shame. Also know that when you get to the shore, you can sit down with your journal and write down all the things that you figured out so carefully while you were in the healthy shame boat.

So now look to your right or to your left and choose one direction—maybe one of the shores is rocky, the other shore is sandy, or one has a dock, and the other has kind of a soft landing. Allow this drifting boat—this boat that kind of guides itself—to gently, gently move in the direction of one of the shores. Notice how it just guides itself over to one side. You don't have to steer or guide it; it just follows some amazing flow of nature. And, being in the boat, you're in that flow too.

Release any shame or judgment or darkness and just allow the transformation of healthy shame to take root deep inside you—in your bones, in your heart, in your soul. When the boat lands where it wants to land, allow yourself to climb out. Thank the boat, and maybe sit down on the bank for a while to journal, enjoy the beautiful day, and appreciate such a wonderful boat. If you want, you can leave it there, or you can push it off down the river.

Bring yourself back to the present moment and take some time to journal about your experience.

## Kind Inner Coach

Imagine a coach who you know or have worked with who is truly kind. If you can't think of one, imagine a character like this from a movie or book. Who could speak to you in a kind and encouraging voice? Now gently recall something from your past in which you did something you wish you hadn't or you long ago decided that you did wrong. Imagine you could change what you did. Pretend the past is like a movie or play that you can return to and move the actors around in according to your wishes. Now imagine your kind inner coach hands you a new script with entirely new lines than the ones you followed or said before. What do the lines say? How do you behave differently? Whatever it is, imagine that you receive the reaction you wish you would've had if you'd gotten everything right the first time. Really feel what it would be like to have the memory changed so you come out with a win.

## Healthy Shame Journaling

This practice resembles the exercises at the end of the last couple of chapters. Begin this one with the same type of grounding session by breathing in and out at your own pace. See if you can make your exhale just a little longer than the in-breath. Then put your hand on your heart and say, *This breath is all I need to observe and not react.* Let yourself breathe naturally for a few minutes. Then, with hand on heart, say, *This courage is all I need right now.*

Now imagine that above your head, a string connects you to the sky and pulls you up. There's also a string under you that connects you to the ground and pulls your energy safely to the earth. Breathe in the energy of courage and breathe out the messiness of shame binds. Breathe in courage, breathe out shame. You don't have to fix anything. Just begin to notice whatever thoughts and feelings and emotions came up as you were reading this chapter and thinking about your life and experience with shame. Continue to meditate for five minutes or so, and then consider the following:

Healthy shame is intimately connected to having solid internal and external boundaries. Many who experience toxic shame have a challenging relationship with boundaries. Growing your awareness of boundaries can help grow a little healthy shame, even if establishing boundaries may feel odd or uncomfortable at first. What is your relationship with boundaries? Are you aware of any shame associated with boundaries? Feel free to write down your answers and reflections in your journal:

> *I notice . . .*
>
> *I also notice . . .*
>
> *I wish I could have changed . . .*
>
> *I can't let go of feeling . . .*
>
> *I wish I could tell someone . . .*

At this point, it may help to say to yourself, *I hear you now. I am here with you now. I care about your feelings.*

Is there something you have felt shame about for a long time? Have you been abiding by some rule or agreement that you have to keep your anger inside? Was there ever anger you had to hold back to protect your family or others?

> *I notice . . .*
>
> *I also notice . . .*
>
> *I wish I could have changed . . .*
>
> *I can't let go of feeling . . .*
>
> *I wish I could tell someone . . .*

Let yourself know that your feelings are welcome here.

Now contemplate your relationship with joy and fun. Does shame ever get in the way of you having fun? How does the shame stop you?

*I notice . . .*

*I also notice . . .*

*I wish I could have changed . . .*

*I can't let go of feeling . . .*

*I wish I could tell someone . . .*

Once more, remind yourself that all of your feelings are welcome.

To finish, take some deep breaths and ask yourself what you might need in this moment. What do you need next? Think about what you've learned from these practices. Begin to see the changes in the way you hold yourself. Give yourself permission to be embodied and to share that in the way you sit, talk, and walk.

As before, if you feel triggered by anything that comes up in this work, take a break, seek comfort from someone you trust, or return to an earlier chapter in this book before moving on.

5

# Shame and Your Inner Child

*You can shame a nine-month-old baby who's got no*
*concept of doing anything wrong . . . The shame predates*
*any wrongdoing.*

—Gabor Maté

Our childhood stays with us. Things that happened to us when we were young—at two, at five, at ten—strongly influence our current life. Though we may develop adult bodies and think our childhood is long behind us, somewhere inside, the child is still alive, directly affecting our thoughts, words, and actions. This is the part of us commonly referred to as the inner child. Shame happens when your inner child is triggered.

Just as a baby or young child is full of life and energy, the inner child carries a great deal of our desires and impulses and life force. It also carries our wounds and disappointments. It may be that the most important relationship we have is the relationship we develop with our inner child. Many adults have moments of sudden sensitivity or confusion that make no sense to them (and others), and they often struggle to set boundaries in relationships because they don't realize how deeply what happened as a child still affects them. Some may deny the inner child part of themselves or even dismiss or criticize it. Unfortunately, when we ignore, deny, or attack our inner child, the result is shame—momentary or constant.

## CHILDHOOD SHAMING

We are not born with shame, but we are born with the ability to feel shame. At some point, we experience a break in attunement and then begin our lifelong experience with shame.

Ed Tronick is a developmental psychologist who wanted to understand the way infants and mothers interact. He devised what's now referred to as the Still-Face Experiment, in which Tronick had mothers play with their baby, make faces, and respond to their child while matching the baby's energy.[1] After a time, the women were instructed to stay with their baby, but to not respond to the child's actions. They were told to keep their face completely still, showing no emotion or connection. While still physically present with their baby, in a real sense they were no longer fully there.

> Most breaks in attunement that happen between children and their parents are unconscious.

At first, the babies tried harder to keep their mother's attention. Their gestures became more emphatic, their smiles wider, and their vocalizations louder. When that didn't work, the babies began to protest by frowning, screaming, and clenching their fists. But the mothers were instructed not to respond, and the babies finally stopped trying. They became passive and quiet, their expressions and posture going blank. There are videos of these experiments available on YouTube, and they're disturbing to watch. Thankfully, that's not where the experiments ended. The mothers were instructed to interact and play with their child again and, after a few moments, their baby would respond and come back to life as before.

We interpret the collapsed state the babies went into as a physiological and emotional state of shame. The mothers had purposefully frozen themselves and stopped interacting for the sake of the experiment. It's clear that doing so was painful for them, and they gratefully resumed contact. Unfortunately, most breaks in attunement that happen between children and their parents are unconscious. Often parents aren't even aware there's been a break, so how would they think to repair it? And when children get a little older and experience breaks like these, the meaning they typically make is that the disconnection was their fault. This results in deep-seated notions of oneself as *bad, wrong,* or *harmful.* These breaks in attunement vary in severity. Children can be ignored, casually shamed with off-handed words, punished harshly, or—at the far end of the spectrum—physically or sexually abused.

## SHAME IS THE BEST POSSIBLE SOLUTION TO AN IMPOSSIBLE SITUATION

Holding ourselves responsible for the deep pain of disconnection prevents us from feeling the utter powerlessness of knowing that something is terribly wrong and there's nothing we can do about it. If there's something wrong with *us*, there's a chance we'll be able to change or fix it. But as children, we may intuitively know that there's nothing we can do to change adults. It's ironic that shame—a powerless state—originates as a solution to an even greater experience of powerlessness.

> Our most enduring and profound shame comes when a current incident triggers something we were shamed for as a child.

In one way or the other, we've all been shamed as children—unconsciously or consciously, occasionally or frequently, in small ways or large. As children, we are especially dependent on adults and especially prone to shame, and we don't yet possess the capacity to modify our feelings and emotional reactions. When there's a break in attunement—*Mommy isn't there in the way she normally is; Daddy's angry; somebody I really care about and trust is criticizing me*—we feel absolutely terrible. It really hurts. Breaks in attunement can be major sources of shame for children, even when adults don't recognize that anything is wrong.

## TOXIC SHAME COMES FROM BOUNDARY VIOLATIONS

Whether a boundary violation is small or quite traumatic, it must be recognized and repaired in order for it not to generate lasting shame. The bigger the violation and the younger the child is, the more painful the feeling of shame in being invaded or abandoned will be. When such a rift occurs, the child seeks to make sense of it all by taking the blame and seeking out ways to adapt their behavior and needs. Children might understand that parents are at fault when they're much older, but they can still suffer from the unconscious belief that something is wrong with them. The younger the child, the more embodied this belief becomes.

As the Gabor Maté quote that opens this chapter suggests, infants can experience shame well before their cognitive capabilities come online. And as evidenced in Tronick's study, the physiology of shame (pulling in, freezing up, withdrawing, and so forth) can occur well before children are able to put thoughts to what's happening. We could call what happens in infancy *pre-shame* because full shame only sets in with the belief that there's something wrong with us—a belief that takes root and determines our perception of the world into adulthood.

As we referenced with the 90/10 Split in chapter 1, real-time situations in the present can certainly shame us, but our most enduring and profound shame comes when a current incident triggers something we were shamed for as a child and our inner child becomes triggered.

The connection might be completely unconscious to our adult mind, but the inner child knows. For this reason, discovering what from our past is being triggered by a present interaction is vital in understanding, coping with, and mitigating our shame.

## NEGLECT

As noted above, when people think about childhood shaming, they often think of severe criticism or physical punishment of some sort, but neglect is every bit as powerful. As children, we have many needs, and attention may be the most important among them. In the 1950s, when John Bowlby (the founder of Attachment Theory) was doing his work, hospitals were paying a lot of attention to cleanliness. This was true especially in units that took care of babies. Hospitals were so afraid of germs that nurses were only supposed to touch babies while feeding or cleaning them, and mothers were only allowed to visit their sick babies once a day. Many hospitals didn't allow parental visits at all.

It may be hard to believe, but hospitals followed these "no touch" and "no visitor" policies in the US as recently as a few decades ago. After setting up these rules to keep the babies from catching illness through germs, the hospitals were surprised by the number of babies who were lethargic and losing weight. The babies were *failing to thrive*, in hospital lingo. Germs weren't harming the babies; lack of attention was.

James Robertson, one of Bowlby's disciples, started a crusade to convince hospitals to let nurses pick up and cuddle babies and give them motherly attention. Robertson encountered lots of resistance but prevailed in the end. Nurses were instructed to make physical contact with the babies, parents were allowed to visit more often, and the infant mortality rate plummeted.[2]

There are also situations that lead to neglect that are partially or completely out of a parent's control, such as a parent needing to be hospitalized or leaving the family for a job or because of a divorce. The child will often blame themselves for the parent's absence and feel that it is somehow their fault. We have also had many clients who still carried shame from a time when extra attention was given to a new sibling and they felt left out, especially if the sibling had special needs.

If our need for attention and basic caretaking isn't met as we age, we begin to think that there's something wrong with our needs and that we can't expect anyone to care or deal with them. Just needing physical contact or psychological comfort or even something as basic as food may begin to feel shameful. Over time, the shame can easily progress to feeling defective just for having the need, but the need remains central to an adult's life. They may attempt to have it met by the wrong people, or the need may go underground and be denied altogether.

## ANGER

Children need to have their emotions acknowledged and accepted as real and important—including difficult emotions, like anger, grief, and fear. This can prove difficult for parents if they're not comfortable with the emotion expressed. Some adults have trouble dealing with any emotion at all and therefore shame their children with punishment, criticism, dismissal, or even ridicule. The emotion that's hardest for many parents is anger.

### A Student's Experience of Getting Angry

As a child, when I was angry with my parents, I was sent to my room. I could return when I was "ready to behave." When I came out of my room, we just moved on. I behaved. I don't recall processing the situation or my anger. There was no guidance on how to improve my expression. While I was in my room, I talked to my counter-shaming dog. I stayed in my room as long as it took to contain my anger and prepare to act in agreement with my parents. The timeout was beneficial in allowing energy to abate, given we had no other strategies. I don't believe we resourced ourselves to process emotions. We simply moved forward with a fractured bridge. This process was my parents' best attempt to improve upon their own childhoods, which were subjected to absence, alcoholic rages, and emotional illiteracy—an improvement, and yet the process was lacking. The impact was that I didn't learn skills to express my feelings of disappointment, upset, or anger. My approach was to register my anger internally and presume I was not allowed to express it lest the bridge be broken. ☀

### How Bret Hid His Anger

My parents were both well-meaning but wrapped up in their own pain and always fighting. They pushed each other's shame buttons. My father didn't come home for days at a time, and my mother was constantly waiting for him and trying to please him. When he did come home, they would fight. In the pictures I have of myself as a child, until I was seven or so, I look thin and either sad or angry. But in the pictures of me after seven, I've gained ten or fifteen pounds and have a somewhat forced smile on my face. That fake smile stayed with me for years. People liked it. They thought I was happy all the time.

In my thirties, I was in a Reichian therapy group, and several people in it pointed out that I was always smiling and that it didn't seem genuine to them. So, I decided to work on it and learned to drop the smile. Later, however, I was in a group in which someone made an offhanded and dismissive comment about me. I felt nothing and stayed quiet. My best friend in the group leaned over and whispered, "Your smile is back." I forced myself to let go of the smile, and almost immediately I could feel my face change and my anger surge forward. I realized that this was the anger I'd been holding back for years.

My parents neglected me in a number of ways—they were too busy, my father was gone from the house, my mother was too depressed to make dinner, and so on. Whatever it was, I wasn't supposed to get angry or complain. And so I learned to hide my sadness and anger behind that smile. ☀

## MULTIGENERATIONAL TRANSMISSION

In most cases, parents aren't consciously cruel. They're just lost in their own struggles, or they simply don't know how to meet their child's needs. In some cases, however, parents are actively causing harm, often by responding to their own shame by shaming the child.

### From Father to Son

Sheila worked with a couple in which the wife complained that her husband was berating her son, screaming at the boy and calling him a wuss for not trying out for sports at school. As Sheila worked with the husband, he revealed that he'd been severely bullied by other kids when he was in high school for not being athletic or sports oriented. His childhood shame was now evoked and being placed on his high-school-aged son. Once the man realized what was happening, he was able to calm down and become more accepting and supportive, no longer unconsciously transferring his shame to his son.

We refer to this as the *multigenerational transmission* of shame. Shame gets passed down from parent to child and then to that child's children later on. We are dedicated to stopping this transmission. The motto we try to instill in our students and our clients is as follows:

> *The buck stops here. I will explore and understand my own shame so I don't transfer it to my children. I will be aware when I shame them anyway because I get triggered or by not being available, missing their cues, or setting rules and boundaries—and I will always try to make repair.*

When children differ from their parents in interests, temperament, gender preferences, and other ways, parents may experience more trouble navigating those differences and react with shaming. Sometimes the differences point to something in ourselves that was unacceptable for some reason or didn't fit into our own parents' vision of who we should be or what we should look like, resulting in tacit or overt rejection—at least of certain parts of us.

### A Client's Reflection

Growing up, my sister was very feminine in a traditional way. She liked to wear dresses, play with dolls, and do all that girlie stuff. Me? Not so much. I liked to roughhouse, play in the dirt, and build forts, so everybody made fun of me for being a tomboy. I didn't know what that meant; I was just being myself. The teasing got worse the older I became. Even my family would make comments about the clothes I preferred to wear, how I cut my hair, how I talked, and so on. It wasn't until I left home and found people who accepted and loved me for who I was *just as I was* that I realized how hurtful my childhood had been. Even to this day, the shame of being so different in my family still lingers.

## IT'S NOT JUST PARENTS

Parents and guardians aren't the only source of childhood shame and shaming. Other relatives—including siblings—can contribute to shaming, as can teachers and peers. Some of the worst shaming happens with such people, and the less supported and met a child is at home, the more shame they may feel in negative interactions elsewhere. We work with clients who still feel shame from a teacher's mocking criticism decades later. And difficulties with friends or peers as a preteen or teenager can produce shame that an adult feels for the rest of their life.

### A Painful Memory

As a teenager, Talia loved to ice-skate. At some point, she became good enough to be invited to take part in a local performance. She was overjoyed and couldn't believe she'd been selected to play one of the leads, and Talia was starting to feel good about her body for the first time—she was thin, but strong and athletic, and her body felt *right* on the ice. Plus, she had so much fun wearing the costumes with glitter and being a part of the ice-skating team. Unfortunately, on the opening night of the performance, just as Talia made her big entrance, a boy in the crowd shouted, "Look at that fatty!" Talia was so stunned and hurt that she almost couldn't skate. She managed to continue and finish the performance, but the pain of that boy's shaming stayed with her for years.

Such cruelty is all too common in the preteen and teenage years. Sadly, it can leave lasting scars. In trying to fit in and adjust to all the social and physical changes, everyone feels shame, and it's all too easy to try to soothe yourself by shaming somebody else.

## SOCIETAL SHAMING

One of the main sources of shame and shaming comes from the inability to handle difference. Some of the most severe shaming that occurs is the product of deep flaws in society itself in accepting and valuing differences. This strongly affects people of minority ethnic groups as well as people with disabilities, nonconforming gender identities, and political or religious beliefs that are not the community norm. The more rigid and limited the social norm, the greater the shame.

### Sheila's Experience with an Evolving Family

A few years ago, I was working with a family that had several teenagers. The mom told me that her daughter had recently sat her down and said, "I need to tell you something. You've always thought of me as your daughter, and I really need you to think of me as your son." The mother admitted that at first she was shocked—she kept trying to figure out if she'd done something wrong or if her kid's change was about growing up without a male father figure in the house. I helped her notice all the reactions that were coming up and reminded her how much of a role shame was playing in it all.

In time, the mother was able to approach her son with more curiosity and openness, which led to him sharing websites of other kids who'd publicized their trans journeys, as well as the mother finding a PFLAG workshop to help her better attend the needs of her child. Eventually, she learned how to advocate for her son at school and beyond: a new driver's license and passport, a new school ID that also reflected his new name and gender, a gender-neutral restroom at school . . . All of this took an unbelievable amount of time and dedication, all while the mother was still adjusting to her child's changes, as well as her own feelings about them.

Of course, these weren't the only challenges the family faced. The boy's siblings were also experiencing shame about the transition, namely about attending family gatherings and not wanting to deal with extended family members' reactions to what their sibling was going through. They just wanted a "normal" family who didn't have to deal with such difficult feelings and experiences of difference. All of them were dealing with the shame society places upon people who are different—especially the ones who dare to show who they truly are.

We've known a number of clients who have experienced intense social shaming because of the color of their skin, their stuttering, their sexual orientation, or their having a different religion or a lack of religious belief. Needless to say, some societies favor certain ethnic groups above others, which results in discrimination for children at school and elsewhere. The resultant shaming can affect them deeply, even if their parents provide a strong sense of belonging. And this societal shaming can continue into adulthood. One of the most difficult tasks, even for the best parents and guardians, comes in helping their children become resilient in the face of the societal shaming that may come at them from various directions and may very well become a lifelong experience.

### Bret on Being Jewish

My father's father changed our family name so we wouldn't be easily identified as Jewish. When she was a kid, my mother lost a close friendship with a girl who came home from church one day and screamed at my mother, "You killed Jesus!" and never talked to her again. I've always taken pride in my Jewish heritage, and even though I've never had to experience the discrimination and shaming that my grandfather and mother did, I've definitely had a few experiences (for example, being cursed at for being Jewish) that have really stung. ☀

We're both acutely aware that far too many people today face discrimination, exclusion, and shaming that is ongoing, intense, and even dangerous. We work with clients and students of various ethnicities, ages, and identities who come from a wide range of upbringings and social environments. While we always try to find common ground with our clients and students, we also strive to acknowledge, discuss, and respect the differences in our upbringings, religious beliefs, values, and social experiences.

### Sheila's Work in Foster Care

Many years ago, when I was working at a foster care agency, one of the foster parents took me aside to explain why some Black parents are so strict and disciplined with their boys. She said, "We have to be tough on them. If we don't, how are they ever going to be ready to deal with the police?" Her point was that what seemed like harsh treatment on the outside was really all about love and protection, but I couldn't fully grasp what she was trying to tell me until the shocking cases of George Floyd, Michael Brown, Eric Garner, Tamir Rice, and far too many others were made public in the past few years. ☀

## NECESSARY SHAMING

Just as shame is a primary emotion that can't be eliminated, neither can we get rid of the act of shaming. In the process of raising and socializing children, parents need to set boundaries and teach appropriate behaviors, which means that some form of shaming is inevitable. There will undoubtedly be breaks in the interpersonal bridge.

As Donald Winnicott states in *Playing and Reality*, children can benefit from manageable interpersonal ruptures as long as their parents are attuned to them at least a third of the time.[3] Winnicott's work was a huge relief to mothers all over the Western world, as mothers have too often been faulted by psychology for just about everything that happens with their children. Indeed, there's no way to be a perfect mother, perfect father, or perfect caregiver of any sort. All we need to strive for is to be *good enough*. As we emphasized before, the awareness and acceptance of our limitations are vitally important in counter-shaming ourselves for our inevitable weaknesses, mistakes, and less-than-ideal decisions.

It's not a matter of *if* we will shame our children in the process of raising them, but *how*. Just as we want to transform our experience of shame, we want to transform how we enact shaming. Just as we believe that there can be healthy shame, we believe that there can be healthy shaming. We see the key to parenting—as well as to any successful relationship—in the three Rs: Relationship, Rupture, Repair.

## THE THREE R'S: RELATIONSHIP, RUPTURE, REPAIR

Imagine that a mother notices that her child has run off the sidewalk in front of their house and is now playing right in the middle of a city street. In alarm, she screams, "Johnny, get back here right now!" stamping her foot and waving her arms for emphasis. Johnny, startled and scared by his mother's response, immediately runs back to her.

When we ask our students to picture this scenario, they disagree as to whether this is an example of good or bad shaming. Clearly, the interpersonal bridge has been broken, and we can see the effect of that in Johnny's reaction. In truth, we can't tell yet if this is toxic or healthy shaming. That all depends on what comes next. Does she punish him and call him stupid? Or does Johnny's mother clearly express her worry, tell him about the danger he was putting himself in, and give him a hug? The process of small rupture and fairly quick repair over time can make the interpersonal bridge even stronger.

Just as there's healthy shame, there's also healthy shaming. There are times in every relationship that we have to say *no*, times when we need to set boundaries and limits, times when we must tell other people that they're doing something hurtful or wrong. And that message may affect them with shame whether we want it to or not. Relationships become ruptured at times—interpersonal bridges become broken—but they can also be repaired.

One of the marks of toxic shaming is that there's not a lot of concern with how the other person responds to it. In fact, if the other person gets upset, the person doing the shaming often gets annoyed and responds with something like, "Oh, get over it. You're too sensitive." How many of us have heard messages like this from people we care about? First, we get shamed, and then we're shamed again for how we respond to being shamed.

> It's so meaningful when children receive heartfelt apologies from adults.

For this reason, we want to learn how to recognize when there's a rupture and approach repair with awareness and care. In a relationship between two adults, this might sound something like, "I'm sorry that I hurt you in my flailing around. I was trying to maintain my boundaries and ask for what I needed, and I didn't do it very well. Can we make a repair?" In Johnny's case, that might look like his mother acknowledging how scared she became and saying, "I'm sorry, Johnny. I was just so scared that you were going to get hurt. I love you so much, and it means the world to me to know that you feel loved and safe." It's so meaningful when children receive heartfelt apologies from adults. Not only does it open the door to more trust in the relationship, but it also shows them how to practice healthy shaming themselves.

It's also important to break the pattern of shaming yourself when you recognize that your efforts at healthy shaming aren't perfect.

Kindness and self-forgiveness are crucial here. Healthy shaming is often hard to do in the moment, but you can always go back later and make the best repair with yourself or others that you can.

## THE INNER CHILD AND THE ADULT

When the interpersonal bridge is broken often enough or severely enough and that bridge is not repaired, the intrapersonal bridge also gets broken. We become severed from ourselves. We start to doubt ourselves and have shame about our feelings and needs. When there's been enough criticism or neglect from others, we begin to shame ourselves. A part of us takes over the role of the shaming parent or teacher. What was once external shaming is now happening within us.

Even as adults, we have a part of us inside that's still five years old (and eight, and ten, and so on). Those parts still carry the joyful energy, vulnerability, and need for connection they experienced when we were actually that age. They also carry our shame from that time in our lives. Unfortunately, as adults, we often critique or deny those parts of ourselves, which severs the intrapersonal bridge even more.

What adult doesn't occasionally find themselves acting in strange and detrimental ways for seemingly no logical reason? It turns out there is a logical reason, but it comes from the logic of the past. Our inner child's shame has become triggered, and it's taking over our adult nervous system. This is especially true if we have a bad relationship with our inner child and tend to react by shaming or ignoring it. The inner child will do whatever it takes to get our attention.

## INVERSE EMPATHY

It's so important that we learn to listen to our inner child with compassion and understanding. It's also crucial that we learn to have their back. When recalling how their parents violated their boundaries, far too many clients will justify why their parents did it.

### One of Bret's Clients on His Father's Violence

Sure, my father hit us when he was drunk. He used a belt on me. I still have scars. But he had a terrible childhood. His own father left the family when my dad was ten, and he had to become the man of the house. He was working full time by the time he was fifteen. And then he had to support three kids. At least he didn't leave us like his father left him. He may have hit us, but at least he was there.

This is an example of what some call *inverse empathy*. This client was sympathizing with the person who had abused him, rather than the scared hurt boy who had been abused. Sadly, this perpetuates the shaming experience. In this case, it was vitally important for this client to learn to express more compassion for his inner child, who certainly didn't deserve to be beaten black and blue, rather than justify the actions of his abusive father and generate more shame.

## INNER CHILD ERUPTIONS

Strong reactions that are inappropriate to a given situation usually mean that our inner child has been triggered. These eruptions are often accompanied with an Attack-Other response that directs anger from the past at someone in the present moment who typically doesn't deserve it. These reactions frequently occur between lovers and spouses.

### A Client's Inner Child Eruption

I recently lost it with my husband. All he did was ask if I'd paid for our daughter's summer camp, but I felt like he was grilling me and looking down on me for not taking care of basic family business. That's what my dad did when I was a boy. He'd double- and triple-check about the chores I was supposed to do around the house, even making me walk around with him to review my work. It really pissed me off, but it wasn't like I could tell my dad I was angry. That's what gets triggered when my husband asks questions like that, even when they're just neutral requests for information he doesn't have. But if I can stop and realize what's going on—how that little boy in me is getting triggered, old stuff—it takes a little bit of the heat off. And it helps me forgive myself, take more responsibility for my eruptions, and repair the bridge with my husband. ☀

The inner child can also erupt in other ways—impulsive behaviors, like speeding or binge drinking, for example, or shirking responsibilities, like forgetting to pick up their children from school or expecting their parents to support them into adulthood. One of our clients hadn't bothered to file their tax returns for seven years and didn't seem to understand why they were being audited.

## SUPPRESSING THE INNER CHILD

In a society that values production and controlled behavior, people usually don't want to deal with the needs and feelings that their inner child still carries. This is often true because those particular needs and feelings were discouraged, ignored, or actively shamed in childhood. Shame about the inner child and the resulting suppression from that shame are key elements that fuel addictions. Most addictions are created to deny feelings and needs that may not be accepted or met. This is the Deny reaction we described in chapter 3.

To counter this denial and suppression, some people dealing with addiction recite the Serenity Prayer; they remind themselves to take their lives one day at a time, or they rely on the counter-shaming structure of an honest and supportive community. In Overeaters Anonymous, the question *What am I eating not to feel?* is used to promote more self-awareness.

### Joanie's Struggles with Her Addiction

Joanie was addicted to opioids. She relayed her story to me with very little emotion, and when I (Sheila) asked her to share her feelings more, she refused. After working together for a while, I reminded Joanie that the feelings and needs she didn't want to talk about were coming from her inner child and that her inner child needed her. Could Joanie hold that little girl for a while? Could she tell her that everything was going to be okay? "No," Joanie said. "It's not going to be okay, and I hate my inner child. I don't want to deal with all of her messy emotions and stupid needs." Over time, I was able to persuade Joanie that her inner child needed her, and eventually Joanie started to open up and even cry from time to time. The turning point in our work was when she agreed to let me help her hold and care for her inner child. As we worked with her inner child, her addiction faded away.

## A LOVING RELATIONSHIP WITH YOUR INNER CHILD

If you were regularly shamed growing up—whether by your parents, siblings, classmates, or others—it can take a lot of hard work to create a loving relationship with your inner child. The effort is more than worth it, however, as we've seen countless times with our clients and students. Here's how one of our students describes the healthy, loving relationship she has worked hard to establish with her inner child:

### A Student's Weakness, and Her Strength

Around the time I was five years old, my shame and trauma shifted me into excessive self-control. Reflecting on this now, I notice a sensation of sadness in my body. While I have experienced deep layers of healing and growth in my own life, when I think about my five-year-old self shifting into this, I feel sad for the many experiences of childhood joy and delight she lost or missed out on because of doing so. However, I can also acknowledge the resourcefulness of this response at such a young age. The sadness in my body moves into tiredness when I reflect on the number of years this excessive self-control required such energy and effort on my part. No wonder I've been so tired for most of my life. Now I'm able to acknowledge the tendency for excessive self-control that still exists within me. I see it. I know what caused it. I see how it has impacted me. I see how it kept me safe and helped me become successful. I also see that it no longer serves me, and I have the ability and awareness to more easily notice when I step back into those old patterns. I also have the skills to bring myself back into a natural space of pendulation, not having to control myself all the time. It's not perfect, but it's so much better.

## PRACTICE

### Taking Care of Your Inner Child

This is a multistep exercise that will help you put into practice some of the things we've covered in this chapter. To start, simply close your eyes, take some breaths, and let yourself feel your heart. Imagine radiant energy around your heart. Grow into it, expand it a little. Breathe in the hope and breathe out shame; breathe in peace and breathe out shame.

Take some moments to remember a time recently when you felt stuck or went blank and let yourself think back to when something similar happened in childhood. Let yourself watch the movie of that memory and review what happened when you were shamed. Then imagine traveling back into the movie now and choosing one thing to make different. If you wish, you can bring someone bigger than you to protect you while you change the power dynamic. What did you want to say that you were too ashamed to say at the time? Imagine you can say it now. See the other person's reaction as you do so.

Let yourself read these words and realize that this is part of working through the mystery of your relationship to shame, especially when you feel stuck or your inner child becomes triggered. And know that the information in this chapter can be vital and potentially life-changing. That being said, it can also be confusing or threatening to some parts of us, so it's important to be wise and gentle with kind mindfulness as you try the next steps.

If it's available to you, find a quiet space to sit with yourself. Bring a journal and a favorite pen and glass of water too. Take a sip of water and say to yourself, *This sip is all I need for a deeper part of me to process what I've read in this chapter. I'm inviting this deeper part of myself to symbolically hold my hand as I drink the water.* Then close your eyes for a couple of minutes and feel yourself breathing in and breathing out. If you have a regular mindfulness practice, you can use that now to bring yourself to a grounded place. Take some deep breaths in, each for the count of nine, and breathe out each of them to the count of ten, so the outbreath is just a little bit longer than the inbreath. Now say, *I'm good enough for today.*

Next, imagine that a wise person is coming to witness you. Know that at any time you can stop and go back to any part in the book you'd like to revisit and write down anything that comes up. Listen for the small voice inside, that inner critic who wants to put you down for one thing or the other. For now, simply welcome it. Let yourself write down whatever comes to mind, the positive and the negative. You could allow yourself to write down the inner critic's negative messages for a page or two, but then stop. Remind yourself that some of it—if not most—simply isn't true. Then tear those pages up.

Next, turn to another page in your journal and find a different small voice that wants to tell you all sorts of positive things about yourself, even though another part of you feels flawed. These parts can coexist. You can still let the light in. Imagine now that you're visited again by a wise and compassionate person—let's call her your inner mother. What does she do? What is her face like? What does she want to do to re-mother those hurt young parts of you?

If you feel ready for another next step in this practice, stand in front of a mirror and put your hand over your heart. Tell yourself, *I love you.* Notice your eyes in the mirror. Do you detect any changes? Just pause now and take a long breath with your eyes closed. Then open your eyes and say to yourself, again, *I love you.* Doing this, you might notice some negative chatter come up from your inner critic. It might be trying to pull you back into shame or the shame binds we've discussed in the book. Just witness this happening and remind yourself that the work you're doing now will ensure that small changes happen over time. Every major transformation is made of small changes just like this.

Finally, come back to your journal. Make a page or section just for discoveries. What did you notice while exploring this practice? How have shame-bind experiences played out in your life? How do they continue to shape your view of the world? All your feelings are welcome here. On another page, list out any inner-child emotions you notice. How would you like others to respond to them? What would you like people to say? Lastly, conclude the practice with some deep, mindful breaths and by telling yourself, *I'm okay. I'm good enough.*

6

# Healing Your Inner Child

*It's never too late to have a happy childhood.*

—attributed to Tom Robbins (and various others)

We are all born with powerful imaginal resources. We can easily visualize or think of people, places, and things that have never existed in our everyday reality. Children learn to cope with life largely through play and fantasy. As we get older, we may use this ability less and less, but it remains with us regardless. Our imagination not only makes life more interesting, it also helps us survive.

Along with their exuberance and lack of social conditioning, children have a rich imaginal life that helps them create games, play with friends who others might not see, and wholeheartedly believe in the existence of Santa Claus, the Tooth Fairy, and their favorite superheroes. They haven't yet made a clear division between their imaginal world and what most of us call *reality*. This can sometimes prove challenging for parents, who are often up to their necks in the responsibilities of making a living and keeping up a household in that reality. For this reason, parents can unfortunately treat imagination as a silly waste of time. They might occasionally pretend to listen to the latest shenanigans of their child's imaginary friend, but the interest isn't sincere, and far too often parents will simply ignore, dismiss, or criticize children for their imaginative play. This is why children eventually experience and talk about the imaginal realm less and less the older they get, until they, too, are almost completely severed from that world.

Reality is nowhere near as real as we pretend it is. Our notion and experience of it are formed by our preconceptions, by what we've been trained to see. Birds can see colors and dogs can hear sounds that are completely inaccessible to humans. Additionally, scientists have long demonstrated that our senses aren't passive recipients of the external world; we usually only perceive what is interesting, dangerous, or of use to us.

When we're adults, our perceptual field might be significantly reduced, and we may have cut off most of our connection with the imaginal realm, but things haven't changed at all for our inner child. In a sense, the inner child itself is an imaginal concept, but that doesn't make it any less real. So, to benefit our inner child—as well as our more adult parts—we need to allow ourselves to spend quality time in our imaginations. In the imaginal realm, logic and time and meaning are fluid and flexible. What this means is that what occurred to us in "real" life—everything that remains stuck in the cognitive realm—can be explored and changed in our imagination. In this way, we can revisit and resolve shaming situations from our past.

> What occurred to us in "real" life—everything that remains stuck in the cognitive realm—can be explored and changed in our imagination.

## THE FOUR REALMS OF EXPERIENCE

We have postulated four ways (or *realms of experience*) that people receive and process information:

- Cognitive (thoughts and beliefs)
- Somatic-emotional (feelings and sensations)
- Interpersonal (relationships with others)
- Imaginal (dreams, possibilities, and images)

Much of this book addresses the cognitive realm because we want to reframe the way you think about shame so shame can assume it's place as an important and useful part of your life. We're also giving you hands-on information about how to change your relationship with shame, and most of that fits in the cognitive realm as well. But in order to truly transform shame, we have to utilize all the realms. This is a lot easier to do with in-person workshops and therapeutic sessions, but the practices and personal stories we've placed in the book are also intended to help you activate your somatic-emotional, interpersonal, and imaginal realms. To rewire our nervous system and transform shame, we need to be precise and clear about what happened in our past, learn to be okay feeling all our feelings, and to exercise compassion for ourselves and others. Additionally, we need to open and utilize our imagination.

Even as adults, we spend much of our time in the imaginal realm. Anytime we think about the future—and much of the time when we think about the past—our imagination is in charge. We think about things that haven't happened yet and will most likely never happen, and much of the time, we remember events in ways that don't coincide with what actually happened. Since imagination is such an important part of our lives, we need to learn to acknowledge and utilize it as children do. That is the aim of this chapter: to offer you some imaginal tools to help you on your journey to healthy shame.

## HOLD LOVING CONVERSATIONS WITH YOUR INNER CHILD

As with any healthy and rewarding relationship, listening and sharing are crucial. Keep in mind that the shame voice—that inner critic of yours—is often an interject of one or more of your parents or other caregivers. The part of you that feels the shame, on the other hand, is your inner child. For this reason, take great care in how you relate to your inner child and be sure to shield them from any shaming messages your inner critic might feel compelled to deliver.

### A Student Listens

I have simply practiced slowing down, listening, and enjoying the beauty around me. In these moments, the little voice of the pre-shamed me can speak about her desires. I can't hear most of what she is saying yet, but I've succeeded in creating enough internal space that I am finally hearing the voice.

## CHECKING IN WITH YOUR INNER CHILD

Set up time to listen to your inner child regularly—once a day or once a week, for example. Get a status report on how they're doing. Listen with caring and kindness and imagine that you're with a young version of you—perhaps a five- or eight-year-old version. Over time, this practice will bring you closer to your inner child, and you will learn to trust each other. After you listen and gain their trust, you can reassure them and tell them about some of the good things you're planning for the two of you. You might find that your inner child isn't always what you suppose: they might end up being way more feisty, gentle, brave, or creative than you expected.

## IMAGINAL RESOURCES

One of the striking aspects of being a child is how little choice we have. While we can live large in our imagination, we spend a lot of time—at home, at school, and so on—doing what other people tell us to. Once we consciously reenter the imaginal realm as adults, we suddenly have lots of choices. We control the scenario. We decide who's included, who to leave out, and the fates of everyone involved.

We covered resourcing earlier in the book. Sadly, most of us don't have anywhere close to the number and quality of resources we'd like in everyday reality. In the imaginal realm, however, we can create an abundance of resources—an overabundance if we'd like. We can call on anyone to support us in our imagination, and we're not limited to the people we've known in real life. Of course, if we've known a person or pet who did help us or who loved us unconditionally, that's great. We can call them up in the imaginal realm, even if they died a long time ago. And we can also call upon other support from characters from history, from our favorite stories, from movies, or completely from our imagination. We can once again enjoy the company of an imaginary friend who is devoted to us or an imaginary protector, who can help shield us from all harm, protecting us with fierceness. We can likewise call upon a kind and wise inner coach whose job it is to advise us and help us solve problems in life.

## FIND A PROTECTOR

When working with children, it can be helpful to offer a basket of toys—including small plastic monsters—and ask them to pick the scariest thing in there to take on the role of the negative voice that's been plaguing them. After listening to the monster speak for a while (and defending the child from its criticisms), we transform the creature from a critic to a protector from other negative comments or put-downs. For children who've never experienced protection, this can be a wonderful new experience.

### Jerry Finds a Protector

Jerry had trouble receiving his wife's criticisms. Eventually, he realized that whenever his wife spoke, Jerry was hearing the vicious voice of his mother when he was a young boy. I (Sheila) offered him the same plastic figures I use with children—superheroes, dragons, dinosaurs, regular-looking people, and some mythical creatures thrown in for good measure (including a Bigfoot). Jerry and I had a good laugh about me asking him to play with them, and I acknowledged his feeling that it was pretty silly for a grown man to do. Jerry chose the Bigfoot figure to use, and I persuaded him to imagine that the Bigfoot wanted to be his protector against his hurtful mother. Surprisingly, it worked. Jerry was able to suspend his disbelief as he imagined the Bigfoot roaring at his mom and telling her not to put little Jerry down or else the Bigfoot would bite her! He took a deep breath for the first time in the session. Jerry had felt alone for much of his life, and this session was one of the few times he'd felt like he had a real protector.

## DEVELOP A KIND INNER COACH

When exercising our imagination in this work, people are often afraid to let loose because they don't want to come across as silly, foolish, or not good enough. Understandably, they don't want to feel more shame in the process of working with their shame. When this happens, we like to invite them into a playful space by asking them who their favorite superhero is (or *was* when they were a child). The superhero can serve as a protector. They can also serve as a kind inner coach. It's common that clients will consider this sort of exploration a waste of time. Aren't we supposed to be doing hard work on shame? And isn't hard work supposed to be serious?

A kind inner coach can nurture your inner child as they struggle with shame. Your version doesn't have to be a superhero of course. As mentioned before, some people choose wise people they've known in real life or guides from literature and history. Feel free to try different options and find one that works just right for you.

## TAKE THE HERO'S JOURNEY

In the imaginal realm, we can assume any role we'd like. One role it's often helpful to assume is that of the hero—the one who chooses a meaningful quest or journey. And because all the great quests of literature and film include helping spirts, guides, and teachers of some sort, it's a good idea to include these in your imagination as well.

### Sheila's Client and the Buddha

Years ago, when I was working as an eating disorder specialist at a hospital, I had a particular client who came to a therapeutic group and helped everyone there, but nothing I did seemed to help her. She told me that she'd done something unforgivable and that she didn't deserve to eat or live. What was working for everyone else in the group wasn't reaching her, so I decided to call on a higher authority.

I noticed how tightly she held her body with her arms and legs crossed. I asked everyone in the group to draw a circle in the middle of a piece of paper and then write something secret and unforgivable in the center of that circle. Then I instructed them to fold the paper in half and then fold it again and again until the paper was as small as they could make it. Throughout this process, I watched how tightly she held that piece of paper.

I led a guided visualization for them to imagine holding this tightly folded, vitally important piece of paper in their hands while they saw themselves walking out of the door, down the street, and into the woods. Then I asked them to imagine holding the paper as they walked all the way through the woods until it became sandy and turned into a desert. Then they were to keep walking with the paper in the blazing sun with no food and no water, but they were somehow still able to continue across this vast desert. And far ahead, almost as far as they could see, was a little hut. And in that hut, there would be someone who could take the paper from them—a holy person, perhaps, or maybe a kindly grandparent—and forgive them for whatever terrible thing they'd written on their piece of paper. After that, I instructed them to take the same path back, all the way back to where we were sitting in circle in the room.

When the group came back and opened their eyes, other members were looking at this woman and pointing at her emphatically. She was breathless and practically jumping out of her chair with excitement. When I asked her what happened, with amazement and joy, she said, "Sheila, it was the Buddha! The Buddha was in the hut, and he forgave me!" This is how we found her higher authority—the one powerful being who could convince her that she deserved to eat, that she deserved to live.

It's important to note that work like this is somatically grounded (in the above example, the heat of the desert, the exhaustion of trudging on one step at a time with no food and no water, the feel of the piece of paper in the hand). It's also crucial to keep in mind that some techniques work better than others. Affirmations from higher authorities might work for you, but they might not. If you can find a way to combine the somatic realm with the imaginal realm, you can create something far more powerful and lasting in helping change your self-image, the roles you assume in life, and your behaviors.

## EXPAND YOUR ROLE REPERTOIRE

In *Acting for Real: Drama Therapy Process, Technique, and Performance*, Renée Emunah writes, "Our self-image determines our repertoire of roles, and our repertoire of roles determines our self-image."[1] If we expand the roles we're capable of playing in life, our self-esteem grows exponentially. Conversely, the more self-esteem we enjoy, we naturally find more roles to express in life. Shame stands in the way of those roles as well as our self-image.

Examples of self-images include *I'm the smart one, I'm alone,* and *Nothing good ever happens for me.* The self-image we carry comes from a lifetime of events—some pleasant and positive, some not so much. Our self-image is also partially inherited from our family's history—

maybe they experienced oppression of some sort, financial hardship, or significant privilege. Our families also have a lot of say in the roles we end up playing in life.

Drama Therapy pioneer Robert Landy asserted that the self is a composite of different roles based on interaction with family and community members.[2] In other words, all of us are a fluid collection of roles. Some are more prominent than others for survival or self-expression, and our roles can become fixed when we grow up in a rigid or enmeshed family structure. That's how we get stuck playing roles like the *good girl*, the *hero*, the *outcast*, or the *lost child*.

### Diana's New Role

I (Sheila) had a client who regularly ducked her head and went into the shame posture when anything new happened to her. When I invited her to explore why this might be, she recalled the certain hateful energy of a bully in high school. Part of our ongoing work together involved her imagining other roles she could take with the bully—a protector, for example. This was appropriate because there hadn't been anyone there to protect her as a teenager. I asked if she could imagine protecting her inner teen now that she wasn't alone anymore, and the idea for the new role came together in a beautiful way. She imagined putting on cowboy boots and kicking that bully in high school out of her life. And then the stuckness she carried of being in the victim role with all its accompanying shame was replaced with a new role of an energetic cheerleader who was a supportive and fun counter-shaming influence. My client's imagination naturally called up these roles, whereas I myself often use Quan Yin (a goddess of compassion) or Athena (a goddess of wisdom and warfare). When he was a boy, Bret identified with Captain Marvel Jr., but now as an adult, he envisions Abraham Lincoln for his courage, perseverance, and integrity. ☀

## FIND A NEW STORY

A life story, or coherent narrative, is how we make sense of our lives. If there's enough toxic shame around, our whole life story gets simplified into *I'm bad* or *There's something wrong with me* or *It's all my (or someone else's) fault*. Our real story is much more complicated than that. We want to replace the overly simplified and painful narrative created by toxic shame with a much more accurate, precise, and complex narrative—one with a lot more discernment, that sees more of the details, recognizes the grays, and can glimpse the big picture. This is what healthy shame empowers us to do.

The cross-generational transmission of shame and trauma needs to be transformed or the narrative of that shame and trauma will continue to the next generation and the next and the next, as well as out into others in the world we share. This means it's up to all of us to transform our stories with kindness. In this way, there's hope for a world governed less by shame and more by love and connection. Shame is the compost for a new narrative. Compost is usually made up of a lot of things we don't want around anymore—rotting fruit, molding leaves, used coffee grounds, and so on—but that compost is what makes new growth (including food that nourishes us and others) possible.

### *"I Should Have Been"*

When Sheila first met this client, the client was frustrated and depressed. She kept saying, "I really blew it. I should have been a doctor! That's what my parents wanted. What's wrong with me?" Her inner critic was constantly putting her down and shaming her for not following her parent's dreams and plans for who they wanted her to become. They weren't even pressuring her anymore; she was the one who was still giving herself a hard time. Her self-image was being attacked by an inner bully. Sheila noticed that the voice sounded young. Sheila asked how old she was when the doctor decision was made for her. Quite young, as it turns out—too young to have been able to decide what she really wanted out of life.

Sheila invited her to enter the imaginal realm and talk to that young part of her. As we did so, new ideas began to emerge. The woman began to understand that her inner child had felt bullied by her parents and believed that she had to hide her true self this entire time. Gradually, her inner child was able to open up, creatively express her desires, and move beyond this long-standing, toxic anger-shame bind. Over time, she created a new story that said nothing was wrong with her and that sometimes dreams take a while to emerge, and before long, she was actively exploring what her soul purpose was. The new story she had adopted for herself was magnificent.

## GIVE BACK THE SHAME

When we ask clients and students to come up with an image for their shame, some feel it as a darkness, void, or black hole inside them. Others describe it as something external—an ooze or slime that covers them, for example. We believe that these images come from being shamed by the words and actions of others. To counter these powerful visualizations and sensations, we've come up with an imaginal technique for giving back the shame that was put on us.

We believe that this *giving back* needs to be done in the imaginal realm. There may be occasions to confront others for what they've done and said to us, but this is a separate process and needs to be done quite differently. And even if such were to occur, the confrontation with those people will prove much more useful and effective after completing the imaginal process. In the imaginal realm, we can do or say anything without being concerned about how it will affect another person. Our imagination is our own private realm. When we are communicating with others, on the other hand, we are in the interpersonal realm. In that realm, we do need to take account of the other person—both how our communication will affect them and how their reactions will affect us. Thinking your boss is an idiot is perfectly fine. Telling your boss that they're an idiot could get you fired. There's a crucial distinction between self-expression and communication. In the imaginal realm, anything is private and acceptable. In the interpersonal realm, there are major limitations as we consider the feelings and reactions of other people.

To a lot of people—particularly those with a distant or hostile relationship with their inner child—all this imaginal work can seem frivolous. It might be silly sometimes, but in truth it is extremely powerful in tangible ways. The unconscious does not fully comprehend the difference between the imaginal realm and everyday life, and this is especially true if the fantasy experience employs a somatic base. As with dreams, what feels real can have lasting effects in what we typically call "real" life.

### Audrey Gives Back the Shame

I remember being around nine or ten years old and going with my best friend to the ice-skating rink. I had never ice-skated before, and she was very good. She had promised to teach me, and I was looking forward to it. After a couple of missed attempts, I finally managed to get on my feet and skate around slowly, feeling like Bambi. There were a lot of kids on the ice that day, some of them skating very fast. At some point, I fell (in the middle of the rink) and couldn't get up. I tried to, but just couldn't. My friend was laughing at me, not helping me. She just skated in circles around me, laughing while I—more and more clumsily—tried to get on my feet again. I remember not wearing gloves and being petrified that any of the fast skaters who were swooshing by would cut off my fingers. I remember crabbing my way to the side of the rink on all fours, feeling so embarrassed and humiliated. And let down by my best friend. I'd just wanted her to smile at me and lend me a hand. I wanted her to encourage me and tell me I was doing great and that she would be there for me all the time.

Working with Bret and Sheila, I imagined revisiting that experience as a fire-spewing dragon. I felt empowered and strong, and every cocky kid who laughed at me that day now looked at me with utmost respect. In dragon form, I looked at my friend directly in her eyes and said, "What the fuck is wrong with you? Why did you treat me like that? Why didn't you help me? What kind of pathetic friend would behave like that? Fuck off, loser. I don't need you as my friend."

But after I got those feelings of revenge out of my system, I gained a new, healing revelation about what had happened. I was able to see a bigger picture. I understood that my friend had done that to me because I was the brightest student in our class together; finally, she had something she was better at than me. She couldn't resist taking advantage of the moment.

Very often, as we help people in this process, they gain new insights about the bigger picture, especially about the shame of the shamer. In most cases, the person who shamed us was awash in shame themselves. They shamed us as part of an Attack-Other reaction, trying desperately to get rid of their own shame by putting it where it didn't belong.

We have found this imaginal process to be incredibly freeing, but it can also come with a lot of sadness about what happened because our grief is no longer bound up with our shame. But once our grief begins to come into the open and voice itself, we're better able to tell ourselves a new story and—as with the client who imagined herself as a dragon—gain new life and vitality as a result. That's what happens when the shame and righteous anger that have been bottled up for so long are released.

This process can help us rewrite the past and give our nervous system a new story to process. We can transform what happened, or fill in the gaps of what was missing, and then reengage with life in more nourishing ways. We can create better boundaries, prioritize healthy relationships, and support ourselves and others more optimally. We can tell our truth and express our righteous anger too.

That being said, the student above was trained in our work and had lots of resources to bring to the process. While imaginal work like this can be done on your own—especially when it comes to incidents that weren't physically threatening and don't involve parents, guardians, or close relatives—we highly recommend having someone there to help you, ideally a professional who has experience working with shame. Mostly this is to manage any backlash that might arise for you. Additionally, if you are someone who can have trouble distinguishing between fantasy and reality, we strongly recommend against doing this work on your own.

> We need to extend more compassion to our inner child and allow them the freedom to express righteous and justified anger about what happened to them.

## AVOID BACKLASH

Whenever we talk about giving back the shame to others, there's frequently someone who finds the idea shocking. "By getting revenge, aren't we just shaming the person who shamed us? Doesn't that make us just like them?" This is an understandable reaction, especially if you have been brought up with a strict religious or moral code. If this is the case for you, there's a strong chance you'll experience a backlash when you do this work and feel that you're just as bad as (if not worse than) the person who originally shamed you.

The distinction is that you were shamed in real time, whereas you give back the shame in the imaginal realm. In psychological terms, you're not working with actual people but with introjects. When shaming remains external, it can affect us without taking over, but we often internalize the shame in the form of introjects who exist inside of us in the imaginal realm. Those are the parts of us we're giving the shame back to, not actual people.

Earlier, we talked about inverse empathy—when we feel more compassion for the person who shamed us than we do for ourselves.

We need to extend more compassion to our inner child—to all the parts of us that were wounded—and allow them the freedom to express righteous and justified anger about what happened to them. Doing so, we aren't hurting anybody; we're actually freeing ourselves.

## CONFRONTING PARENTS AND CAREGIVERS

As powerful as public shaming by friends can be, chronic abuse or neglect by our parents and caregivers is often more damaging. For one thing, shaming from these people usually begins when we are younger, far more dependent, have fewer resources, and even less agency and choice. Additionally, the shaming that comes from parents and caregivers is often longer in duration, stretching on throughout our childhoods and even long into adulthood. To make matters worse, these are the people we need and love the most. Their words and actions have a weight that others don't carry.

Unfortunately, when people begin to process their shame in therapy or support groups, they are sometimes motivated to confront their parents directly. Therapists have even been known to encourage this. While a direct confrontation may turn out to be useful, it can also result in more alienation and shame. Sometimes the people we wish to confront are no longer available, or the power differential has shifted (the person who was the powerful, shaming parent is now old, frail, and even childlike). As well, the people we wish to confront don't always remember the shaming event, don't possess enough self-awareness to receive what we want to tell them, or are buried in their own experiences of shame. The people we want to confront may become defensive or triggered and speak or act in ways that shame us even more.

When someone has experienced a particularly powerful and painful event, we always stress being *with* the resulting emotion rather than *in* it. People have an either-or tendency with their emotions and child parts—they tend to push them away entirely or let them take over. Some of our clients who have done somatic therapy tend to identify with their feelings and actually lose themselves in them. We have other clients who are deathly afraid of their painful feelings and don't want to go there at all. We suggest going back to the scenes of trauma and shame in the imaginal realm as a full adult, bringing all of your resources with you. That way you can have compassion for what the child went through without having to regress and endure the full onslaught of the painful feelings. You can go back while retaining your capacity to see the big picture, including the fact that you are no longer in that painful situation. And you can confidently tell your inner child that it will get better.

### Barry Confronts His Father

From the age of four, Barry had been shamed and bullied by his father for not being manly enough. He'd grown into a talented and respected artist, but he was still haunted by this childhood experience. Having done years of therapy and somatic work, Barry was ready and eager to feel into that painful memory in order to overcome it. I (Bret) made sure to ground him in the present— connecting Barry with his competence, strengths, successful career, and love of nature. At some point, we began to feel into his memories, but I cautioned Barry to bring all of his strengths and gifts into the past. "Now that you're so resourced, you can be with the child who was so hurt and shamed. You can have compassion for that child."

When Barry confronted his father, he did so as a full adult, standing between his father and the little boy. Looking at his shaking inner child, Barry was saddened and outraged. He turned to his father and said, "How could you? How could you treat a little boy this way? Do you know how much you hurt him? Can you see how stupid and cruel you were? Well, you're never going to mistreat him like that again. I'm going to protect him. And if you ever try to hurt him again, you're going to answer to me." Then Barry thought a moment and said, "No. I'm not going to leave him with you at all. I'm not going to risk it. You don't deserve him. He's a much better person than you'll ever be."

Barry turned to his inner child, who was looking at him with rapt attention and a growing smile, and said, "Let's get out of here. You're never going to have to go back." Then Barry picked up his four-year-old self, cradled the child in his arms, and took him away. The change in Barry was amazing as he came out of his imaginal state. I could see he was full of power and determination, and there was also childlike wonder in his eyes. Barry sat in silence for a while before saying, "I did it, I really did it. I finally got him away from that fucker."

When clients access their righteous anger, it often helps clear some of their shame, but that's certainly not true for everyone. Giving back shame to parents and caregivers is a complex and highly individualized process. For this reason, we like to work gradually, first using the imaginal realm to give back shame to someone who has shamed our client in the present, when they're an adult who's in touch with their resources. We then try to work backward in time until eventually addressing early shaming events. Again, we strongly suggest working with a professional helper who is familiar with this technique.

## THE DANGER OF FORGIVENESS

While we believe that forgiveness can be useful in freeing ourselves from the past, we do not prioritize or encourage it. We see forgiveness as a spiritual process, one that can arise naturally from acknowledging and working on shame, and perhaps with guidance from spiritual and religious beliefs. We are strongly opposed to telling anyone that they "should" forgive abuse or neglect. To us, there's a huge danger in heaping even more shame on the victim—a person who has already been shamed enough. Telling yourself or someone else that they need to forgive someone who hurt them encourages inverse empathy, whereas we believe they should be prioritizing compassion for themselves.

Until we've thoroughly explored our shame, we don't truly know what it is we're forgiving the other person for. Although we teach the importance of understanding that our shamer also carries their own shame, that knowledge is not in service of forgiveness, even if it eventually contributes to that. Seeing how shame works and gets passed down from person to person helps us view the big picture, become clearer, take responsibility where it's appropriate, and move on to healthy shame. Healthy shame can lead to forgiveness, but it doesn't have to. As one of our clients put it, "I'll forgive my mother when I'm damn well ready to, not when somebody tells me to."

You will only feel better if your forgiveness comes when your inner child is willing. And it's crucial that you don't put any timelines on the process or shame yourself even more for not being ready. A healthier goal is to strive for kindness and compassion, and that starts with taking care of your inner child. Ideally, working with your shame and healing from it is all about feeling better in the present, living more fully and joyfully, and facing the future with a more nourishing and positive outlook.

---

## PRACTICE

### Inner Child, Inner Protector

This is a two-part practice. Please begin by grabbing your journal and taking a few deep breaths. Think of a misunderstanding or rupture that happened when you were young. Let your inner child hold your pen or pencil and write. Just a few sentences. Then let your mindful adult read it. After you've done this part, start a new page while imagining that your inner coach says something like, *We are turning to a new page because it's a new time in your life. What do you want or need now that you didn't get when you were younger?* Let your inner child write about this for a few minutes while your inner coach says kind and encouraging words. Your inner coach is also realistic, so they remind you that sometimes things take a little longer than you want them to. Finally, when your inner child is finished writing, the coach says, *Thank you*. Imagine the shame from your past healing a little bit at a time; imagine your inner child feeling listened to, supported, and healed just a little bit more.

The next part of this practice involves an inner protector. As before, begin with a few mindful breaths and then ask your inner child to go back briefly to a time they felt shamed or bullied or dropped in life. Write about that experience for a few minutes. Then read it while you imagine a protector for your inner child. What do they look like? Are they a person you knew growing up, a favorite pet, or some fierce monster? How does it feel to have this protector by your side?

Replay the hurtful scene in your mind and write down what you wish someone would have said or done to protect you. Then listen to your protector say, *This stops here*. Notice what happens next. Maybe you imagine a bully apologizes. Maybe you're not shamed in the first place. Or maybe everything happens as it did before, but you feel stronger and more peaceful about it. How does the protector respond? If there are others involved, how do they react to the presence of your protector? What changes? Write everything down and hear your protector say, *I am here with you now, and I will protect you!* Notice how it feels to be protected, have your dignity restored, feel your self-esteem repaired, and experience so much compassion for your inner child. Write as much down about this experience as you'd like.

Your inner coach or inner protector can take you to the next level in your personal growth. This relationship is very much like making a new friend who you can keep as a resource after this chapter and even long after you've finished this book. They can be like a best friend who watches out for you whenever you need support.

7

# Shame and Trauma

*I have come to the conclusion that human beings are*
*born with an innate capacity to triumph over trauma.*
*I believe not only that trauma is curable, but that the*
*healing process can be a catalyst for profound awakening.*

—Peter Levine

*rauma* was originally a medical term referring to an event that causes
a sudden, intense shock to the body—a physical attack, for example,
or a car accident. More recently, *trauma* has come to mean both the
devasting event and a person's reaction to that event. In this book, we
are focusing on the second definition. The International Association of
Trauma Recovery Coaching has defined *trauma* in the following way:

> Trauma is defined from the perspective of the individual.
> A circumstance or event that might be traumatic for
> one individual might not be for another. Temperament,
> prior experience with trauma, and level of resilience all
> play a significant role in someone's individual response

to a potentially traumatic event or circumstance . . . A circumstance or event is traumatic to an individual if it meets the following three criteria:

1. The person feels they are powerless to control the circumstance or event.

2. It frightens the individual in a substantial way.

3. It changes their beliefs about themselves, the world, and their interactions with the world.[1]

This means that events that may be manageable for adults (such as being shamed or ignored) can more readily prove traumatic for children. To begin with, children have many fewer resources to help them and very little choice.

> While not everyone has experienced trauma, everyone has shame.

Trauma is a reaction to one or several events that overwhelm the nervous system. Shame, on the other hand, is a primary emotion meant to protect us, and it's often the result of repeated incidents over time. While both shame and trauma are reactions to threat, trauma involves an extreme threat of physical harm, even death. It can also involve an event quite outside of normal human experience. As we've explained, the threat that produces shame is a threat to connection and belonging. While not everyone has experienced trauma, everyone has shame.

As we indicated in the chapter on shame binds, we think of trauma as an extreme fear-shame bind that also involves other primary emotions, including grief and anger. Shame is designed to help us lower the intensity of other emotions so we don't act on them. For children, shame binds the anger so we don't angrily lash out at our parents and other caregivers (although we may lash out at other people), and shame binds our grief so we don't reach out and seek solace with others. In trauma, the fear reaction gets stuck in the initial freeze state. Trauma also evokes the startle reaction—the physiological changes that happen when we are suddenly surprised: our shoulders go up, our head jerks back, and our breathing stops in a sharp inhale. People may freeze during this response.

The freeze response of the nervous system is much stronger when trauma accompanies shame. For example, it comes on more suddenly. It also tends to be more global than the freeze response that is involved with shame alone.

While shame is an embodied belief system, trauma happens most strongly on the physical level. Because trauma is a significant disruption to the nervous system, and because it causes such an intense freeze response, we want to explain more fully how the freeze response actually happens.

## POLYVAGAL THEORY AND THE FREEZE RESPONSE

Here is a simplified version of Stephen Porges's Polyvagal Theory: In order to sustain life, the body has two complementary nervous systems—a sympathetic system and a parasympathetic one. The sympathetic system arouses us and prepares our bodies for action; the parasympathetic system calms us down. Both are needed for the body to function properly, and both are connected to every organ in the body through the nervous system. Ideally, there's a balance and collaboration between the two.

Sympathetic arousal can relate to joy and excitement, and it can also relate to fear and anger. The more stressful the situation, the more the sympathetic system comes online, with the most extreme example being when we have to physically run away from a dangerous threat. Later, once we're far away and safe, the parasympathetic system helps us recover and calm down. In some cases, however, the stressor kicks off such a strong degree of arousal that our body cannot cope. To protect our body from a heart attack or other catastrophe, the parasympathetic suddenly comes fully online, overrides the arousal, and shuts everything down. It's like driving a sportscar at incredible speeds and slamming on the brakes with the accelerator still pressed to the floor.

If our body is caught between fight and flight, our nervous system provides us with a third option: freeze. To protect us from extreme danger, the parasympathetic system has an emergency braking response that shuts the whole system down. This shutdown can be momentary and short term. Sometimes an animal that is being threatened or pursued falls down and becomes inert, but if the predator doesn't kill it and walks away, the hunted animal can get up and escape. This is where the expression *playing possum* comes from, as possums are known for their unique defense mechanism. We humans might not utilize it to such degree, but we have a similar defense mechanism as well. Unfortunately, it takes us far longer to come out of our freeze response.

> **Shame and trauma remove us from others and leave us isolated.**

Stephen Porges explains that the vagus is a large nerve that runs through the body. It has two aspects: dorsal (or backside) and ventral (the front). The dorsal vagal runs to all the different organs of the body—it's large, primitive, and resembles the nervous system you find in fish. The ventral vagal connects with the muscles of the face, which is where social engagement takes place. For this reason, humans have the most sensitive and highly developed ventral vagal system in the animal kingdom. It's the dorsal vagal that's responsible for the parasympathetic shutdown and the ventral vagal that brings us back online so we can reconnect with others, largely because our facial muscles (and therefore expressions) start working again. Without the activity of the ventral vagal, it would be difficult to reestablish the interpersonal bridge.[2]

Wilhelm Reich suggested that the unconscious is actually the muscular system of the body.[3] He's widely considered to be the founder of somatic therapy, which is employed to help people get unstuck in their bodies. Because trauma and the body are so connected, it often takes more than talk therapy to see positive results. It takes somatic work to get the ventral vagal working, move trauma through the body, repair the bridge, and move forward. Social engagement also gets the ventral vagal back online and helps us release any freeze response we might be suffering from. Shame and trauma remove us from others and leave us isolated; this sense of separation can only be healed when we're physically and emotionally able to reach out again.

## THE COGNITIVE COMPONENT OF SHAME

As Peter Levine, Bessel van der Kolk, and others have illustrated, much of the successful work in healing trauma tends to have a somatic component; the nervous system needs to release the dorsal vagal freeze. With shame this can also be true, but there's usually a stronger cognitive piece, as shame is regularly accompanied with powerful messages that are all variants of *there's something wrong with me*.

Our culture places high value on wielding power and taking action. Trauma prevents that; in trauma, we feel powerless, and we can't do anything about it. For this reason, most cases of adult trauma in Western society are accompanied by shame. Of course, the feeling of powerlessness can be quite overwhelming for children too. When a parent or caregiver crosses the line and abuses a child or neglects their basic needs—especially in an ongoing way—both the shame of the broken connection and the fear of not being able to survive are evoked. The intense shame experience for the child then becomes traumatic.

## HOW THE BRAIN PROCESSES TRAUMA

Our brain is built to process experience and respond to it with emotions, thoughts, and actions. Trauma disrupts the brain's ability to do so. Ordinarily, when something happens to us, our sensory organs process it and send signals to the brain. The amygdala, at the very base of our brain, receives the signals first and checks for danger. If it perceives danger, the amygdala immediately sends a *focus-on-the-threat-and-do-something-about-it* signal to the body. If the amygdala does not detect danger and is not triggered, the information travels through the hippocampus and limbic system, which respond with emotions. Then the information arrives in the cerebral cortex, which puts it in context, compares it to previous experiences, and makes sense of it. Finally, the incident is stored in our memory and becomes part of our coherent narrative: what occurred, when it happened, and what it all means.

Traumatic events don't travel along this pathway. They happen so quickly or dramatically that the information doesn't pass through the hippocampus, which is the gatekeeper to the whole process. For this reason, trauma doesn't get properly stored in memory. In fact, brain scanning has shown that people with severe childhood trauma have enlarged amygdalae and smaller hippocampi.[4] This makes sense when you keep in mind that it's the amygdala's job to detect threat. Traumatic events often do not become part of our coherent narrative. Rather than assume their appropriate role as part of our past, trauma and shame continue to physiologically exist in a perpetual present, easily retriggered by current experiences. When our shame or trauma becomes triggered, our nervous system responds as if the past event is happening right now. We call this the *Shame-Trauma Bubble*. When something traumatic happens to us, it's as if time stops and part of us remains in that place and time. And when something reminds us of that event, we're immediately back there in a very real sense.[5]

Freud talked about the *repetition compulsion*, in which people keep repeating the same mistakes or getting into the same problems over and over again. We believe this is a sign that people are trying unconsciously to go back to a traumatic or shaming event and change it somehow, but since they can't deal with the event directly, the attempt rarely works. And the trauma and shame remain stuck.

What's called for is a way to integrate the traumatic and shaming events into our memory and larger lives. We need to know on a neurological level that what happened is in the past; it's no longer occurring. We think of this as gaining *optimal distance* from the experience. We can remember it and talk about it in detail, but we are fully aware that we are no longer there. We may even become emotional, but we are no longer overwhelmed or controlled by those emotions. We are *with* the memory, not *in* it. And we are no longer overwhelmed by shame when we share the memory with others because we know that what happened wasn't our fault. We can also unlock any outstanding shame binds with grief or anger and learn how to move on and finally thrive.

### Sheila's Early Training with Her Mother

I've had several decades of training to help heal myself and others, but my real training in life came when I was growing up. I lived in a nice suburb of Chicago. From the outside, it looked like I lived in a normal house with a normal family, but inside, my life was quite threatening and scary. My mother had an undiagnosed mental illness, and it was an ongoing struggle for me to protect myself and my sister. I had to learn at an early age how to manage my mother's controlling energy and respond to her with extraordinary care.

I kept a detailed record of my experiences in a secret notebook, describing all the unusual things my mother did, what worked and what didn't with her, and so on. I made a choice early on to do a good job of it—helping my mom, protecting my sister, and figuring it all out by listening, doing exactly what she said, and otherwise being very quiet and still. That went on for years. I'd wake up every morning and just figure it out. I wasn't sure what was going on, but I knew that it was unique—nobody else at school had a mother like I did. I figured that someday I'd write a book about it all. But despite adapting to the situation, I felt frozen with shame.

I knew my mother needed help. My extended family would say she was crazy, but they never did anything to help her or us, so I continued doing it all by myself, which is how I grew up so hypervigilant. But even though I was so alone in the experience, I always felt that there was a profound sense of grace with me, some kindness around me, like I was surrounded by some energy of light, something telling me to keep on. As if my future was telling me that there's a reason to learn about this so I can help other families someday.

I remember once we were walking down the street in front of the police station, and my mother started to yell at my sister. She was yelling so loudly that we were invited in. They put me, my sister, and my mother in separate rooms. Turning on a tape recorder, a police officer said, "I want to help you girls, but you have to answer some questions." And then she asked us, more than once, "Does your mother hit you?" I looked down in shame. "Does your mother hit you?" Well, my mother did a lot of unusual things to us, but she never hit us. And I kept waiting for the police officer to ask a different question, like "Does your mother terrorize you?" or "Does she withhold food because she wants you to write letters for her to your father's boss calling your father crazy?" "Does she cover every surface of the house with newspapers or boxes?" "Is the kitchen closed because of bubonic plague?" "Does she threaten to turn on the gas if someone found out?" or something like that, but those questions never came. I couldn't answer the one question the officer was asking because our mother had never actually hit me. I thought that if the officer couldn't ask the right questions, she didn't really have a clue about what was going on, and so she couldn't possibly protect me and my sister. The officer wasn't asking the right questions—and I was frozen in shame. She didn't know how to help. No one did.

I finally ran away a couple of months before I turned eighteen. I made a deal with my sister that she'd stay with our mom for at least three months when I left before she went to go live with our dad. I figured I needed at least three months head start to begin college so my mother wouldn't come after me and try to ruin everything, like she had for my dad at his job. And then my sister could get out of there too. Which she did. We both got out of there. 🌅

When I share what my childhood was like in our workshops, many students are shocked that I survived and that I'm standing here as an accomplished therapist and teacher. How could I have had such a childhood? Well I did, and I survived and thrived. I'm sharing my story to heal the shame of the secrecy that I kept for so long, to shine light on the darkness and isolation of childhood trauma, and to inspire others to tell their story and heal their shame. I couldn't tell anybody then, but I can now.

My story is unusual, but reminiscent of many others in which children who have been traumatized persevere, seek help at some point, and find a way to move forward and become thriving adults, regardless of their childhood challenges. It's also a reminder that even those of us with extensive shame and trauma backgrounds can keep seeking help, learn how to unbind our shame, escape the Shame-Trauma Bubble, and go on to encourage the same in others.

## GETTING OUT OF THE SHAME-TRAUMA BUBBLE

Sheila's experience with childhood trauma, combined with her training in Drama Therapy, led her to develop the concept of the Shame-Trauma Bubble and to our mission of helping people to come out of the bubble and hold trauma at an optimal distance. We can escape the Shame-Trauma Bubble. It can become an experience in our past that we can remember, talk about, and share with others without feeling like we're stuck in time and frozen again. There will always be residue, and the pain will still revisit us from time to time. But it will no longer have the power to drag us back to experience it all over again or recreate it in the present moment. Recovery isn't an easy process, and it often requires a lot of help, but it's entirely possible.

We employ a number of steps to help our students and clients move into healthy shame. Some of these have already been discussed to some extent, but it's worth looking at them again in this context to understand how they contribute to freeing oneself from the stuckness caused by shame and trauma. As you read through these next few pages, please remember

to check in with yourself, exercise compassion, and take breaks as you
need them.

## Remember That It's Not Your Fault

The first step is to let go of any shame you may carry about having
trauma. In *Good Will Hunting*, the title character in the film is a severely
shamed and traumatized young man who also happens to be a genius.
He meets a caring therapist named Sean, someone Will finds difficult to
manipulate and intellectually run circles around. In the most emotional
scene of the movie, Will's defenses begin to crumble when he starts
talking about his brutal childhood:

> **Will:** He [my father] used to just put a belt, a stick, and a
> wrench on the kitchen table and say, "Choose."
> **Sean:** Well, I gotta go with the belt there.
> **Will:** I used to go with the wrench.
> **Sean:** Why the wrench?
> **Will:** Cause fuck him, that's why.[6]

After a long pause, the therapist turns to Will and says, "It's not
your fault." Embarrassed at his vulnerability, Will deflects. Sean keeps
repeating, "It's not your fault." He tells Will this repeatedly, until finally
the young man breaks down and cries.

> Not being met with a caring connection
> after a traumatic event will evoke even
> more shame and trauma.

When we have been shamed and traumatized as a child, we often
carry the belief that it was our fault. It's vital to understand that it wasn't.
Something happened to us; our nervous system froze. We didn't choose any
of it; it happened *to* us. Sometimes, trauma comes from events or injuries
over which we had no control—a severe illness or home-destroying flood,

for example. But we weren't the ones who caused that to happen. It was something from the outside that disrupted our interior in a significant and lasting way. If the trauma was caused by another person, they were acting out an Attack-Other reaction to their own shame. They were trying to get rid of their shame by passing it on to us. It's their shame, not ours.

## Share Your Story

Not being met with a caring connection after a traumatic event will evoke even more shame and trauma. It's so important to be able to tell your story and have others receive it compassionately. If the situation is bad enough and the shame is great enough, children feel that they have no one to rely on—no one they can tell, no one to protect them, no one to even believe what they have to say. For many of our clients who have reached out to someone during or after trauma, the worst trauma results from not being seen, heard, or believed. If the original shame and trauma is from being invaded physically or sexually, that shame and trauma is then compounded by being abandoned. People can carry even more anger and resentment for the people who ignored them and didn't protect them than those who abused them.

If we weren't listened to as children, we may very well decide that there's no point in speaking up at all, especially about our traumatic experiences. But shame and trauma thrive on secrecy, which makes it all the more important that we tell our story. Of course, we need to use discernment in how we tell it, when we do so, and who we tell it to. It's also important that we don't convey our story in such a way that we become overwhelmed with the original shame or trauma. And it's crucial that we're mindful of who we tell, as many people haven't worked through their own shame and trauma and may become uncomfortable and therefore say or do shaming things as a result. That's why it's a good idea to start by telling one person, someone who can listen with acceptance and care, someone who has the ability to help us keep some distance from it. This needs to be someone compassionate and caring who, ideally, knows about shame and trauma. Over time, we become more accustomed to sharing our story. We are better able to observe the events and details from a safe distance while remaining grounded in the present moment.

## Pay Attention to How It Ended

Trauma often gets locked away in a protective bubble of memory. In real time, the traumatic event ended a long time ago, even if it can feel like it's happening in the present moment. For this reason, we need to explore the moment when the trauma ended because that will begin to break the bubble and integrate the traumatic event into the rest of our life.

### Bret's Client Who Ended His Abuse

Bob carried the shame of having been molested by an older boy. When I asked when and how the abuse stopped, Bob said that the older boy had moved away. Even that information was important because Bob was aware of when the abuse ended. However, something didn't feel right, so I asked where the boy had moved. It turned out the boy had moved just a few miles away from where he had lived before. He was still close enough to come over. Bob had actually told the boy, several months before the boy moved, that he wanted to stop and to not come to his house again. In the blur of time, Bob still vividly remembered the traumatic experience, but he had forgotten his role in ending it.

It's important to remember that as a child, we have neither the power nor the responsibility to control adults. It's also crucial to remember how the abuse finally ended and any actions we did take to survive or change the situation—a situation that's now in the past.

Even when a child does take a strong action to stop abuse, they may feel shame for what they did.

### Steve's Elegant Self-Protection

Steve had the experience as a child of his father occasionally picking him up and throwing him against the wall. It's not only traumatic to be physically manhandled like that; it also produces shame.

Remember that one of the definitions of shame is being treated as an object. That's what Steve had felt like as a kid—he wasn't a child, but something that could be picked up and thrown.

But Steve also developed a strategy to protect himself. He joined the wrestling team when he was a teenager, and a year or so later, when his father started to physically abuse him, Steve used a wrestling technique to take his father down to the ground and hold him there. But Steve felt shame about that too. He felt terrible that he'd done that to his father.

Steve's solution to the abuse was actually quite creative and elegant. To help him understand that, I (Bret) invited Steve to wrestle me to the ground in slow-motion. In the process, I was able to show Steve that he hadn't hurt his father, he'd merely controlled him in order to stop further abuse. Which is when it all stopped, of course, because his father never touched him again. Steve did this at fourteen because he had learned technique. He didn't have to wait until he was bigger and stronger to physically confront his father. And he did it with neither person getting hurt.

Reframing all this for Steve helped him come up with a new narrative. By acting out his protective action, he was able to undo the shame and trauma through careful movements, which produced the incredibly positive feeling of him taking effective action and exercising his personal power. In addition, he could finally let go of the old story that what he'd done to his father was wrong.

## Find and Evoke Self-Protective Responses

For a child, the most appropriate response to the kind of abuse described above is to tell (or threaten to tell) someone who can help you. However, children often feel that there's nobody safe to tell, or they are too frozen in shame to do so. Additionally, sometimes the danger they face is simply too great. Their nervous systems have fully gone into shame as the self-protective response, and they believe everything that happens is their fault.

Older children often develop strategies to fight (as in Steve's case) or flee (as in Sheila's). However, sometimes those self-protective responses become blocked, and the inability to fight or flee can continue into adulthood. It may be hard for someone years later to feel anger or even know how to remove themselves from a bad situation. On the other hand, some trauma survivors react either by habitually expressing anger or constantly running away in a desperate attempt to overcome what they endured in childhood.

In those cases, a lot of healing work can be done in the imagination because, as we've noted before, it's difficult for the unconscious to distinguish between the real world and what's happening in the imaginal realm. This is especially true for children, who will spend hours talking to an imaginary friend or fighting imaginary enemies. As we get older, we're socialized by Western society to separate out the imagination, distrust it, and diminish its importance. From our perspective, this is a huge loss, just as our loss of physical play is as adults. When it comes to shame and trauma, it's truly helpful both to liberate our imaginations and to get our bodies moving again.

## Expand Your Window of Tolerance

Dan Siegel came up with the idea of our *window of tolerance*, which refers to our zone of arousal in which we feel most comfortable and perform best. When we're in our window of tolerance, we learn better, feel better, and relate to ourselves and others in an optimal way. Some of us have windows that can hold more stress, and some of us are more capable when our nervous system is less activated.[7] Whatever our individual case may be, we can all benefit from expanding our window of tolerance.

The process of compassionately dipping in and out of our shame and trauma has a way of expanding the window of tolerance. With our clients, we make a verbal contract with them by saying, "No matter what, I won't leave you there alone in your experience of shame or trauma. I will help bring you back out. I'll be here to help you pendulate." Without outside support, it is much more difficult to work through our shame and trauma in an effective way. We need to work slowly and carefully. If the shame is too painful, we'll simply avoid it or cover it over with drugs, alcohol, gaming, work, or other addictions. That might help us escape for a little while, but it tends to make things worse in the long run, and it does nothing to help us learn to tolerate more pain in the future.

If a river becomes narrower over time, what needs to move downstream will eventually become stuck. Our work, in a sense, is to widen that river (or window) so everything flows better and what needs to move through can do so. We're designed to handle all sorts of painful experiences, but when our window of tolerance is small (or becomes smaller due to our experience of shame and trauma), we're easily overwhelmed. We can't tolerate our feelings because they've taken over. By expanding the window of tolerance, we have more room to go up and down that river, we have more room to float, and we can come back to shore whenever we'd like.

## Transform Your Story and Build a New Coherent Narrative

Shame and trauma form a powerful narrative, one that tells us, *Everything that happened is because I am defective*, and/or, *I have no control about what happens to me and around me.* This is the narrative that leads to hopelessness and despair. For this reason, it's vital to replace that coherent narrative with a more complex and accurate one—one that includes our limitations and our power, our strengths and our weaknesses, the good things that have happened to us, as well as the bad.

---

# PRACTICES

## Resourcing

If it's available to you, find a comfortable place to sit and take off your shoes to feel the ground beneath your feet. Close your eyes, notice your breathing, and really feel how the air moves in and out of your body. Next, think of a time or place where you felt truly good, happy, and peaceful. Visualize where you were and what was around you. Try to recall as many sensations as you can. What did you see, hear, and feel? Just take some time to be there with that memory and breathe.

As you sit there in this lovely place, remember a person who really cared about or supported you or a person you had tender feelings for. You could also choose someone from TV, literature, or film, or someone famous from history; just choose somebody you feel connected to in a positive way. Imagine that person sitting with you in this place. What do they look like? What might they say to you? Visualize all of this as if it were happening in the present moment.

After you've enjoyed this person's company for a while, say your goodbyes to them and then once more find yourself alone in your pleasant, safe place. Stay there for as long as you'd like. When you're ready to end the practice, feel your feet on the ground (or some part of your body on your chair or cushion) and open your eyes. Reorient yourself by looking around and seeing what's around you.

Moshé Feldenkrais developed a system of working with the body called Awareness Through Movement. Feldenkrais was interested in the reeducation of the nervous system, which is what we're after when it comes to releasing shame and trauma. The following practice uses physical movement to do just that.

## Pushing and Releasing

If it's available, find a comfortable spot to sit and feel your feet on the ground. Notice your breathing. Now press one heel very lightly into the ground (either heel is fine) and slowly release the pressure. Repeat this action several times. What's your breathing like as you perform this movement? Do you tend to breathe in as you press the heel down and then breathe out as you let it go? Or maybe you like to breathe out as you let the heel down and bring air back into your body as you let it go. This pressing can be a small movement. The smaller the better. If you do find a correlation between this small action and your breathing, try to reverse the relationship (for example, if you inhaled when you pushed your heel down, try exhaling instead).

After practicing this for a while, try to make your movements smaller and smaller, until the action is only occurring in your mind. You have the impulse to perform the movement, but you aren't physically acting it out. Over time, this practice helps us remember that impulses come and go and we can choose which ones we want to follow up on and perform physically. Now that your heel has stopped pressing into the ground, notice what's happening with your foot. Now pay attention to the sensations in that leg. Is there any difference between the leg you used for this exercise and the one you didn't? Does one feel heavier or lighter? Tighter or more relaxed?

To continue, you can switch legs and perform the same sequence described above, or you can simply imagine doing so in your mind. Maybe your heel will move a little by itself, but just go over the action in your mind—pressing that heel into the ground, letting it come up, pushing it into the ground again, and once more releasing. Do this several times and make sure you are breathing. As above, notice if your breathing correlates with your imagined movement. Finally, compare how your legs feel again. What's changed? Do they feel more similar now? Quite different?

If this practice goes well for you, try this version: alternate heels—first one, then the other, and then back to the first. As you do this, notice if the movement starts traveling up your legs. Maybe it even goes into your pelvis. Follow the same instructions as above: press, release, alternate, and notice your breathing. After a few minutes of this, just let everything go and pay attention to how you feel. Notice what's happening in your feet, in your legs, in your pelvis, and in your back. Notice if your mood has shifted or if anything else has changed. Let the breath go in and out, and slowly end the exercise.

We learned the concept of *orienting* from Peter Levine. Shame and trauma remove us from the present and latch us to something in our past. For this reason, it's helpful to have practices that orient us to the present moment, which helps pendulate us away from shame and trauma. We can do this by asking ourselves, *Where am I right now?* or *What's going on for me right now?* Ideally, this inquiry brings us back to the present truth of our internal sensations. However, if our current sensations are unpleasant (as they often are when we're experiencing shame and trauma), it can be a better idea to orient to something outside of ourselves.

## Orienting

Keep your eyes open, gently look around, and notice your sur-roundings. If something catches your eye, let your gaze rest on that for a while, and then continue looking around you. You can also do this with the sounds and smells in your environment, with your experience of touch on the ground or in the chair, or the feeling of air entering and leaving your body. Doing this practice thoroughly will orient you to the present moment in an "out of yourself" sort of way. You come out of what was troubling you inside by focusing on external sensations.

Trauma and shame both are tremendous at breaking boundaries; we feel invaded by outside factors, or we're abandoned and left all alone. Part of our task in the healing process is to learn how to maintain boundaries and be able to contain ourselves.

## Containment

You can try this practice by placing your hands on your chest or belly. Feel the sense of being held and contained by your hands, and feel the sense of being held within your body. Feel your feet firmly on the ground, pay attention to your breathing, and really feel your hands holding your body. If you'd like, alternate this sensation with looking out into the room for a moment and then coming back to feeling your hands contain your body and your hands connecting you to the earth.

After trying this for a while, take your arms and gently extend them out, as if you're keeping something at bay without much effort. Notice that your arms create an outer boundary of sorts—all around you, there is something of a circle, within which is "you." Continue to feel your feet on the ground and breathe in and out at your own pace. Remind yourself that you have an area that belongs to you. It's yours. You contain yourself; you are contained.

## Older, Wiser Friend

This next practice is a lot like the "Kind Inner Coach" practice found in chapter 4. If it's available to you, begin by sitting comfortably with both feet on the ground. If you want, take off your shoes to help you feel the ground beneath your feet, to call forth that sense of being grounded. You can keep your eyes open for this one, but leave them somewhat unfocused and just notice your breathing as it travels in and out of your body.

Next, call to mind something that happened in the recent past that was embarrassing or where you felt criticized or put down. Or maybe you did something that you weren't proud of. Now imagine that you're sitting somewhere—a peaceful garden, perhaps—and you're thinking about this time in your past and maybe not feeling so great about it. As you sit there, notice that someone is approaching you and you're a little surprised. You thought you were all by yourself in this garden. And as they approach, you become even more surprised because this person walking your way is somebody you look up to, somebody you admire, but somebody that you've actually never met—maybe even somebody who doesn't exist in this reality. Whoever it is, this is somebody you feel good about, and it's somebody who knows more about life than you do. They're older and wiser and full of kindness.

As this person approaches, you can see that they're smiling. They get closer, look at you, and see that you're upset as you recall whatever brought up the shame for you. Just take that in. Let in their smile as you're sitting there, feeling crappy. Then you hear them say something like, "Yeah, I know, I've been there too. I know some part of what you're feeling. I don't know exactly what you're feeling, but I know enough to tell that it doesn't feel good."

Then this older, wiser friend of yours leans forward and whispers into your ear. Only you can hear what they say to you. Whatever it is, it really helps. Maybe it's a general statement about how things move on, how things change but always work out in the end. Or maybe they just remind you that nobody is perfect, that they're certainly not perfect, and that nobody else is either. Or maybe they say something like, "Yeah, you blew it. You messed up pretty good, and that's okay. That happens. It happened to me; it happens to everybody. It just so happens to be happening to you right now."

Then imagine that the two of you are just sitting there in your spot and you see that they are smiling. After a little while, they talk to you about your experience. "Tell me what you might learn from this," they might say, or, "What did you gain from this experience? I know it was awful, I know it stank, I know some part of you maybe thinks your life is never going to be the same again, but is there something that you can take away from all this? How can this help you grow?" You don't have to answer them right away. You might need to think about this for a while.

Your wise friend lets you know that they'd like to just sit with you for a little bit because they can see that you're not feeling so great. They want to help you feel not so alone and maybe give you some encouragement if they can. So the two of you just hang out together for a while until they say their goodbyes and let you know that they'll be around whenever you might need them in the future. But before they leave, they make sure to say, "Thank you. Thank you for being you, for calling on me, and for working on this. Thank you for growing." And then they go on their way and leave you in your chosen place.

To conclude this practice, stand up if you're able and stretch your arms and legs. Take some deep breaths in, look around the room, and come back to the present moment.

You've read a lot of material up to this point, and no doubt you've thought a lot about your own shame and trauma. This can be a little overwhelming at times and maybe even a little heavy. So, for the last exercise, we'd like to invite you to imagine something a little different.

## Kind Hands

Pay attention to your breathing as the air enters and leaves your body. Bring to mind the image of a child—an exuberant, carefree, and innocent child who doesn't have a care in the world. They're just running around, skipping, and jumping, and they're full of joy and delight. Maybe you envision a child you know—a grandchild, say, or a young niece or nephew. Just picture this kid and their happiness and lightness as clearly as possible.

Next, the child walks up to you, and you can really feel the kindness, openness, and brightness of their presence. Imagine that they're standing right in front of you and that you reach out to them gently with both hands, as if you were about to place your hands on the child's face and send them all the love and kindness you could give them. And just as you're about to do that, your hands reach up to touch your own face instead. Notice how your breathing feels now and notice the sensations of your face as your hands are lovingly placed there. What thoughts come up for you? What's this experience like? Just feel what's going on with your hands on your face, breathing in the sensations, and after a moment, let your face know that you're about to remove your hands. Then slowly remove your hands and bring them gently to rest in your lap.

Pay attention to any sensations that have been woken up by this movement. Are there any memories that come up for you? Any shame? Any sense of being undeserving of all that love and compassion? Whatever it is, simply greet it and remind yourself that all feelings and sensations are welcome here. After a few moments of paying attention like this, come back to the present moment wherever you are, and journal for a little bit. What did you feel toward the child? What did you feel toward your face, toward yourself? Write down the details of your experience.

Some people find these sorts of practices to be nourishing and nurturing, but sometimes they can be upsetting or triggering. It's not uncommon to have unpleasant memories arise or to feel awash in shame again. If that happens for you, it might be helpful to remember the older, wiser friend who visited you in one of the practices or perhaps a figure even more powerful, like the Dalai Lama or Quan Yin—the very embodiment of compassion itself. Whoever you choose, take in their good wishes. Feel them there with you, holding your hand and letting you know that everything is going to be okay. Also be sure to take good care of yourself, whatever that means for you, and seek out loving support from people you trust.

8

# Shame and the Body

*To me, the body says what words cannot.*

—Martha Graham

Among other things, this chapter offers some practices to introduce you to your body. That might sound odd given that you are whatever adult age you are while reading this book, but the fact remains that far too many of us have never truly devoted time to get to know our body. Doing so is essential in order to free any shame binds that might be preventing you from feeling your full range of energy, happiness, creativity, and life force.

How can we feel vital and alive in our own skin when shame cuts off pleasure, cuts off experience, cuts off emotion? Our relationship with our body is our first and most important relationship, yet too many of us feel uncomfortable in our own skin. When we're able to live in our bodies instead of hiding from them, we're able to have a healthy, nourishing relationship with ourselves, which enables us to enjoy the same with others.

This chapter focuses on aspects of body image and embodiment, and we will learn to begin to gently talk to ourselves in a kind voice, listening with great care and compassion to all the secret conversations going on inside—conversations that often reveal the perfectionism and shame we carry with us throughout our lives. Transforming the shame in these conversations can lead to a substantial boost in our life force and to living authentically and fully. As you're going through this part of the book, remember that you're not alone. We're all in this together; we're all on this healing-shame journey together.

As you read through these anecdotes and try out these practices, we want to make sure to point out that so much of what we believe about our appearance, beliefs, and behavior comes from outside of ourselves—namely, from our family and larger society. From an early age, we're all informed about what we're supposed to feel, what we're supposed to eat, how we're supposed to look, what we're supposed to be able to do, who we're supposed to be, and who we're supposed to love. So much of this centers on our body and our relationship to it.

## A HEALING SYMBOL

We invite you to take a deep breath now and just notice how the air enters and leaves your body. Let yourself relax into the present moment. Even though you're probably doing this practice by yourself, remember that you're not alone—other people are doing the same practice elsewhere, others have used it to help themselves before, and others will do so in the future. Imagine you are in their company and that everyone is engaging with this practice together.

Continue to pay attention to the sensations of your breathing. After a few moments, imagine that a symbol of healing arises in your mind's eye. It could be almost anything—something floating in the air before you, something anchored into the ground, an animal, a tree . . . whatever you imagine, just know that it is a potent symbol of healing. If you'd like, you could even pause here to write or draw the symbol down on a piece of paper for later, but you don't have to. Just visualize that symbol, and feel its power. And after you've felt its presence for a while, pay attention to your breathing once more, come back to the present moment, and take heart in knowing that now you have another resource—whenever you'd like a little extra help or support, call to mind your healing symbol and feel whatever sense of grounding and comfort it brings.

## Caroline Needed a Kind Inner Coach

Caroline came in for a session years ago and said that she felt stuck and empty inside. When we started to uncover some of her internal conversations, she said, "If I want something, that means I'm bad; if I need anything, I'm bad." That voice for her was quite loud, so we looked for ways to reduce the volume of that inner critic who told her she was bad for having wants and needs. When we were able to do that, she said, "Oh, that voice sounds familiar. That's my gymnastics coach from years ago." The coach had encouraged her to spend seven hours every day training and to severely restrict her diet so she could make it to the Olympics, but something happened at the last moment, and the whole team couldn't go after all, so all of my client's hard work and sacrifice had been for nothing. In order to meet this goal that never panned out, she had to work extremely hard to deny herself some basic needs, and it turned out that she was left with a lot of shame and anger as a result. The inner critic had taken on the voice of her coach, who'd made her feel bad for simply wanting to eat and relax, so we switched that voice to a kind inner coach who reminded her that she was good enough and that she could eat as she liked and take time to relax when she needed to. Together, we were able to show her a different perception of herself, not a perception based on mirrors that were of other people's design. Sometimes this is what it takes to learn how to extend kindness toward yourself and relearn how to allow yourself to experience pleasure. ☀

---

## REFLECTION

Is there a part of you that tells you that you don't deserve anything? Maybe it's food, pleasure, relaxation, or a stable relationship. Whatever it might be, write about it in your journal and then think about a kind inner coach or older, wiser friend who can offer you some different messaging about it.

---

### Sheila's Client and His Food

An elderly client of mine couldn't go anywhere without having quick access to food. He filled his backpack, briefcase, and car with snacks so he'd always have something nearby. This was quite a big deal for him, almost as if it were a matter of life and death. When we dug into his past a little bit, he revealed that he'd been the first grandchild in the family, and so he'd been showered with love and attention. They'd also fed him bottle after bottle of sugar water because they wanted a healthy baby. It turns out that his family had come from a country that had suffered from famine, and the memory of that trauma was still very much alive in them. His family had moved to the United States for better opportunities at that time, and he was the first grandchild to survive. My client was a powerful symbol of survival for his family, and he was given sugar water as a token and symbol of love. Later, as he grew up, my client learned to stuff himself in order to feel that love from his family. I said, "You know, you're all grown up now, and your family is all grown up too. Do you think they could forgive you for not having to always drink sugar water and not always having to be in this survival relationship with food?

As far as I can tell, you're thriving, so maybe it's time to let go of all that and find a different relationship with food and your body." It took some time, but we were gradually able to shift that relationship, which was based on early messages from his family that he carried long into adulthood. ☀

# PRACTICES

## Food and Your Family

Are there any traditions or ways that your family tried to feed you that maybe weren't so helpful? What messages did they send you about nourishment and survival? Let yourself journal a little about that. After a few minutes, think of some ways to counter-shame those messages, for example, *I know you were doing your best feeding me like that. I appreciate the love you've shown me. And now I'm going to find a new way to relate to food and my body. I don't need to eat like that anymore.*

## Inner Mirror Body Shame Practice

This is a meditation and journaling exercise. Start by noticing where these short anecdotes and reflections land for you. Notice your breath as it moves in and out of your body, and after a while say to yourself, *I call for a new paradigm. My goal is to be healthy. My goal isn't to be one weight or the other or to look one way or the other; it's simply to be healthy, awesome, and embodied.* Notice how these words land in your body. Does your body welcome them or keep them at bay? Pay attention to any sensations of shame or any messages telling you how you should look and feel.

Other people have put mirrors in front of you your whole life— family members, teachers, coaches, friends, fashion magazines, various sites on the internet . . . Other people have held you to impossible standards and have said shaming comments to you—intentionally or not—and you've had to live with that for a long time. Notice whatever activation arises as you think about this—these expectations and critiques—and let these old shaming messages drop away from you as best as you can. Notice anything you've used to compare yourself with others and just let that inner critic say what it says, but let it drop off of you like a piece of unwanted clothing.

Feel yourself breathe in and out. Notice the sensations that are going on in your body. Now imagine that you're going to create a new mirror—a soul mirror. Your soul mirror has nothing to do with your external appearance but reflects the brilliance and amazingness of your inner light. In the infinity of time and space, everyone has a soul mirror that does this for them, and it has nothing whatsoever to do with any messages you've heard about what you should eat or wear or look like.

If you'd like, draw what your mirror looks like on a piece of paper or in your journal. You could also just remember it in your mind. Now, on the inside of that drawing or visualization—that is, on the reflecting part of the mirror—write down all the wonderful, luscious, and magnificent things your soul mirror reveals about you. Take as long as you'd like to do this step. When you're done with that part, write any negative messages—that is, anything critical you've heard about who you are or what you look like from the world—in the air or space or wall outside of that mirror. In other words, there's a clear separation here: your soul mirror reflects the real you; all the other comments and critiques don't belong there.

## THE PARABLE OF THE LOG

In *Eating in the Light of the Moon*, Anita Johnston writes about the harsh light that most of us shine on ourselves—the harsh light of shame and criticism. In the book, Johnston relays a story about a group of people who are enjoying a picnic on a hillside. Suddenly, the ground begins to rumble and come out from beneath them. There's a rush of water everywhere, and they all scramble for dear life. One of the people reaches out to grab something, and it's a log that's floating nearby in this great torrent of water. She holds onto that log for dear life.

The log is said to represent her relationship to food. People have all sorts of issues with eating—binging, purging, starving, and so on—and quite often other people in their life have no idea what's going on. This woman is doing her best, holding onto that log and trying to survive, while her friends are on the bank shouting at her to let go. "Let go!" they say. "You don't need that log anymore. Just let go and swim back to shore!" But she can't do it. There's no way she can just suddenly let go of the log.[1]

Most of us can't let go of our logs in one decisive action, and we can't just release ourselves from shame like that either. The woman in this example tries a different approach: she relinquishes her grip gently and then grabs hold again. She does this over and over again until she can stay away from the log a little longer each time. After a while, she's treading water nearby and going back to the log when she wants support, and eventually she can swim around the log, go back to it, and before you know it, she can swim around all by herself without relying on the log so much.

But she doesn't just swim back to shore to her friends and say goodbye to that log forever. If she lets the log go entirely and it floats away, what if she needs it again? So she develops this relationship with the log so she can always swim back to it if she gets triggered or shamed about something. That log is always there for her to grab onto for as long as she needs it, but in a more conscious and careful way, because she doesn't need it all the time like she once did. As soon as her anxiety or shame or whatever form of pain she's going through passes, she can let go and swim around on her own again.

Relating to our shame in this way—whatever our individual log looks and feels like—is an excellent way to practice kindness and compassion for ourselves, and therefore others. As Johnston says, the light of the moon is gentle; it offers us a view of ourselves beyond the grim light of criticism and judgment. The log isn't necessarily a bad thing. It's all in how we relate to ourselves with it.

## INNER CONVERSATIONS AND BODY IMAGE

Shame has a lot to say about how we perceive our bodies, especially for those of us who have been strongly enculturated to negatively compare our bodies to others and impossible standards. The gap between what we see in the media and what we see in the mirror is almost always shaming.

We've spoken of introjects earlier in the book. To review, introjects are internal versions of ourselves often based on external messages that relate to our self-esteem. People who suffer from all-pervasive shame, especially about their bodies, typically have some fairly harsh introjects they have to deal with. Shame thrives on secrecy, and the conversations introjects encourage you to have with (and about) yourself aren't always easy to detect, which is why it's so important to surface what these inner critics are saying.

It's helpful to share these conversations with others, if you can. A close friend or therapist can assist you in bringing these messages to the surface so you can more clearly see how society has encouraged you to shame your body. In that way, you can finally establish a different relationship between them.

## PRACTICES

### Origami Bird

For this exercise, close your eyes and have a piece of paper or journal nearby. Imagine that someone—one of us, your inner coach, or perhaps your wise, older friend—is in front of you holding an intricate origami bird. The bird is folded with great care and complexity, and it shines with a golden inner brilliance. There's so much precision in its folds; every part of it reflects both the light and the darkness.

For some of us, it doesn't feel safe or right to give our shame back to where it came from, whether that's our family or general society. But this origami creature is something different. It can take it. There's no amount of shame that can weigh this bird down. Anything that's heavy on your heart can go right into this bird, and it won't bother it one bit. In fact, that's the bird's job, and it's happy to do it. The bird is designed to take on shame. It has its own power, its own flight path. The bird can take on as much shame as you can release—all at once or little by little. So offer it up to this magnificent origami bird that's shining with brilliant gold light.

Once you've done that, imagine that the bird flies away, not encumbered at all. It can fly right out of the frame of your imagination, taking all that shame right along with it. Notice what visualizing that feels like in your body. Do you feel any different? Where? After a few minutes of sensing this, open your eyes and write for a little bit. What just happened for you?

Once you've reached a stopping point, read over what you've written. If anything stands out for you, underline or highlight it somehow. And if there's any shame that comes up while you're doing this—maybe some critique about your body, for example— imagine that the origami bird flies back into the picture. This golden bird has floated back into the screen of your consciousness to take on more of that shame, and then it'll fly away again once it's taken it on.

Repeat this process a few times: you offer the golden bird your shame, it flies away, you write a little about your experience, and it comes right back if any additional shame comes up. You could even intentionally write down a word or sentence about something shameful you don't want to carry any longer, something you really don't want to pass down to your children or students or anyone you know in the next generation. Offer that word or sentence to the bird and imagine that it takes it from you willingly. It doesn't matter what the shame is—an insult, an ongoing criticism about how you look, the way you feel regularly devalued—whatever it is, offer it to this brilliant golden bird. Notice how the origami bird continues to fly off as if the criticisms were no weight for it at all. Notice how willingly the bird comes right back.

There's a particular kind of shame that some of us carry, and that's when we compare our current selves to younger versions of ourselves, whether that's what we look like now or what we can physically do. We used to be able to run ten miles a day or ride our bicycle for incredible distances or focus for hours at a time, and now we just can't. Or we don't look the way we once did. This last practice is especially designed to deal with this brand of shame.

## Deflection Bracelet

Bring to mind whatever shame you feel about not being that former version of yourself. Breathe in and out at your own pace for a while, and then imagine that you're breathing in grace and peace and that you're exhaling all that shame. The visual component of this practice is something you'll imagine on your own body—it's a bracelet of extraordinary power that you can wear on one or both of your arms.

Whatever negative messages come up—either from yourself or from others—this bracelet (or pair of bracelets, if you choose) has the incredible power to deflect those projections and criticisms out into space. Whatever bad shame energy enters your space, the bracelet just shoots it out away from you. Anything that comes up—shame, anger, jealousness, judgments—all of it gets deflected away from you by this amazing bracelet.

This can be easier to imagine when these harmful messages come from outside of ourselves. Other people try to put their projections on us, and the bracelets just deflect them away. But our inner critic might be the one telling us those things and putting us down, especially when we make unreasonable demands that we somehow remain the same person—looking the same, moving the same—that we were in the distant past. In that case, imagine one braceleted arm on your heart and one on your belly. Breathe in and out, in and out, and ask for grace and joy to flow through your hands, through these powerful bracelets, into your body.

What's that like for you? What sensations do you notice? Maybe you can imagine that something powerful has now taken root in your current body and that you now are also full of great power. Continue to breathe mindfully and notice whatever comes up. After a while, bring this practice to a close and write down what you experienced.

Some of these practices will work better for you than others. If any of them bring up difficult feelings to the point where you feel triggered, please be sure to take a break and perhaps go back to a practice that feels more nourishing or easier to do. Maybe you can try other ones later on, but in the end, you can trust what works for you and follow your path at your own pace. That's what it means to take your power back and be who you are in your own, wonderful body.

9

# Sex, Pleasure, and Shame

*Human sexuality includes more than hormones, organs,*
*and orgasms; it runs through the psychic and spiritual*
*ranges of our lives. We experience our sexuality on the*
*spiritual level as a yearning for another person.*

—Lewis B. Smedes

S exuality is a vital, defining part of our identity. We are at our
most vulnerable when we experience sexual feelings, and therefore,
sexuality is where we're most prone to feeling shame. We're also subject
to sexual shaming all our lives, beginning in early childhood when we
are vulnerable to moral judgments from family and society as well as
to boundary violations from those who are older than us. This sexual
shaming continues into our teenage years, when we are confronted
with hormonal changes, over which we have little control, as well as
shaming from peers and a desperate need to fit in. Then it continues
into adulthood, when we seek to balance partnership with the need for
sexual discovery and adventure. There's shaming, too, when our ability

to function sexually diminishes with age and our faces and bodies are no longer as we remember them.

## SEXUALITY AND INFANTS

Babies are, in many ways, devoted to pleasure. They are emotional organisms in general, but one of the feelings they spend a lot of time with is pleasure—they really know how to feel it. Wilhelm Reich, a great and controversial psychiatrist who was the youngest member of Freud's inner circle, is widely considered to be the founder of all modern somatic therapy. Both Freud and Reich noted that babies get pleasure from every part of their body, which Freud called *polymorphous perverse infantile sexuality*—a name that illustrates attitudes toward sex and sensual pleasure in the Victorian age. But Reich broke with Freud on this matter, praising infants for getting this whole pleasure thing right.[1] Their ability to fully experience pleasure coincides with the fact that babies truly know how to breathe. Watching a baby breathe is an amazing experience, as anyone who has paid attention to them can attest. Their belly pops up like a balloon, their chest floats on top like a raft on the ocean, and their whole body moves: their legs, pelvis, everything. This full breath creates energy that increases their ability to feel pleasure.

As we get older, we get shamed by our families and larger society. As a result, our bodies tighten up in what Reich called *armoring*. Our muscles constrict and our breathing contracts in an ongoing physiological manifestation of shame. Reich labeled the social shaming that shuts us down and restricts our natural access to pleasure the *emotional plague*.[2] Unlike bacterial plagues, the emotional plague is passed down from one generation to the next, not necessarily out of any ill will, but because shaming is a normal part of child-rearing. However, as we've noted, the difference between healthy and toxic shame makes all the difference. Toxic shaming shuts us down and separates us from our feelings and desires. Originally, children have access to all sorts of sensuality and pleasure. Over time, shame restricts that access, showing up later in how we sexually behave, perform, and enjoy as adults.

Ideally, sex is a safe place where we can surrender control. When Reich spoke about orgasms, he emphasized the surrender in allowing oceanic waves of pleasure to flow through us, and he believed that most people had never experienced a full, beautiful release of pleasure, simply because their bodies had been entrained to not breathe fully.[3] Being armored is antithetical to experiencing all the pleasure available through sex.

We believe that the underlying factor in all this armoring is shame. That means that part of our journey with sexuality is to learn to let go of toxic shame so we can more fully access our ability to feel sensual pleasure and our sexuality.

## PLEASURE INTERRUPTED

In chapter 2, we offered a definition from Silvan Tomkins, who states that "shame is the interruption of pleasure." It's a simple definition, but quite useful when we think about shame's relationship to sexuality. Remember that the activities that bring us the most pleasure are typically the ones most affected by shame, and the intense pleasure connected with sensuality and sexuality can easily be interrupted by shame.

### Sheila's Clients and Their Triggers

I was working with a couple who got married in their thirties. They really wanted to have children as soon as possible, but they weren't having sex, which is why they came to therapy. At one point, I suggested an exercise to explore why the husband was pulling away sexually, and the wife started shaking her head no. The husband replied, "There, that's it. It's not so much that she's saying no, but that she's shaking her hair while she's doing it." He then realized that his favorite show as a young boy was *Charlie's Angels*, and all the women in the show had beautiful hair. One time his mother came in while he was enjoying the show and turned off the TV. She was just trying to set a boundary with him, but the lasting result was him feeling shamed for watching *Charlie's Angels* and admiring women with luxurious hair. Whatever her intent, just as my client was beginning to experience his sexuality and feelings of pleasure, his mother came in and interrupted that feeling, which he translated as something being wrong with him. Clearly, this incident had a profound impact on him because he was still triggered by it when his wife shook her own beautiful hair. After the couple understood the connection, they could engage in some repair, he could remain in the present moment, and she came up with some ways to say no that weren't so triggering for him.

## THE DEATH OF PLEASURE

Babies have an amazing ability to seek out and experience pleasure. They receive pleasure out of almost everything; any movement or discovery gives them pleasure. We can watch a baby's joy when they first discover they can put their foot into their mouth. As they grow, children retain the ability to seek out and get pleasure. They can get pleasure from every bodily function.

When pleasure is involved, children can be indefatigable. They can beg to hear the same story over and over again. They can wear down a caregiver's resistance when they want a candy or a toy. They can play the same game hour after hour, with the same result. Pleasure is the great motivator. And with the pleasure comes learning. Children learn by playing, and curiosity is a great motivator in play.

Children have access to various kinds of pleasure. There are the quiet, solitary pleasures (the pleasure of swinging or being in nature, for example), and there are more active pleasures (games, rapid movements, and screaming loudly). As we get older, we're taught to *quiet down*. The quiet, receptive pleasures of older children (reading or playing outside away from the house, for example) might be tolerated just fine, but louder, more active pleasures are often forbidden, interrupted, or shamed. We're encouraged to replace pleasure seeking with *dealing with reality*, thinking about the future, and learning to do what's "good" for us. We go to school on a regimented schedule, sit at uncomfortable desks all day, and our allotted playtime diminishes with each passing year. Over time, we learn that following the pleasure principle is immature; continuing to do so as we get older just gets us into trouble.

Some of us are lucky or privileged enough to find a career that gives us pleasure. One of our clients parked cars in a cavernous garage for a living, and he loved the excitement and the sense of accomplishment so much that he said he would've done it for free. Of course, not everyone has that sort of relationship to work, and far too many people are working simply to survive. Additionally, we're not typically encouraged to pursue jobs because they are *fun*, but more because they are lucrative or stable. From an early age, we are taught that growing up in large part means deemphasizing the role that fun and pleasure play in our lives.

Society sends similar messages regarding sexuality. On the one hand, sexuality is used to sell everything from cars to refrigerators, and nowadays there are websites that promote quick sexual gratification with no strings attached. On the other hand, the true acceptance that sexuality and pleasure have a spiritual dimension and are an important part of everyday life is hard to come by.

## A Student's Religious Shame

My conservative Christian culture was deeply bathed in shame around pleasure. Masturbation was a sin. Sex and sexual exploration outside of marriage were sins. There was so much shame around sex that even within marriage, I felt frozen and unable to embrace a sense of freedom and joy. I'm aware that my own sexual abuse as a child has a significant role in this inability to find freedom and joy in sex, but I believe the shame around sex and pleasure in the religious setting had a much deeper impact. I believe the religious rigidity and shame around pleasure and sex intensified my own experience of shame resulting from the abuse. I can certainly see how I armored myself because of things going wrong in my world. The armor itself made it difficult to enjoy sex in my marriage. I was frozen and often disassociated during sex. It took me an extremely long time to learn how to have an orgasm, and I think there was shame even around my inability to climax in my marriage. My husband was kind and gentle. My shame-and-pleasure bind deeply impacted both of us.

Again, as I reflect on this, there's a sadness that I just need to acknowledge. And then there's some anger beginning to show up as well. It too needs to be seen and acknowledged. The religious shame around sex is (to use Freud's word) so perverse! I am angry about how it touched and influenced so many years of my life. It feels good to allow myself this space to be angry. As I take some time to notice the sensation of anger moving through my body, I feel lighter. And that's good. I also now feel aware of pride and a sense of accomplishment of how much I have worked through, shifted, and grown. It feels like a gift I've given to myself to be young, healthy, and, in many ways, come into my prime years of sexual enjoyment as a woman. I'm grateful to be in such a different space with this now, and even if there are lingering layers to continue to process and heal, I'm grateful and proud of the work I've done to get to where I am. I want to acknowledge and honor that.

## BORN TO YAWN

Our society attaches shame to nearly any bodily function. Toilet training is often fraught with shaming, as is masturbation in adolescence. Any attempt a young person makes to self-pleasure or explore their own body (or someone else's body with mutual consent) is frequently a source of painful shaming. Children are often criticized for being too loud, too expressive, or too physically active. Farting and burping—at least in the United States—are usually frowned upon.

Yawning is like this too. Yawning is an efficient way to expel $CO_2$ from our bodies, bring in a nice hit of oxygen, and release tension in the muscles of our face and chest; so, naturally, our society frowns on it. By and large, it's considered rude not to cover your mouth or stifle a yawn outright. For this reason, we have specific yawning guidelines in our workshops: you don't cover your mouth, and you make as much noise as possible. Try this by yourself sometime. You'll be amazed at how pleasurable a full-body yawn can be.

## SEX, GENDER, SHAME, AND DIFFERENCE

As we've written earlier in the book, differences very often lead to shame. Nowhere is this more true than for those with an identity or sexual preference that is outside of the norm. Although norms have fortunately changed over the past couple of decades, far too many people suffer from shame due to this, including older clients who grew up when homosexuality was outlawed in the United States and the psychological community considered anything other than heteronormative behavior to be deviant. Girls are still socialized toward frilliness, and boys are dissuaded from playing with dolls or using makeup. Children who are attracted to someone who isn't societally approved for them regularly hide their feelings, sometimes for years, creating even more separation from their parents, who the children rely on for support.

### Sheila's Client and the Imaginal Realm

My client was a preteen when she realized she was attracted to other girls. She also wanted to keep her hair short—something that roused suspicion in her mother, who she was sure she couldn't discuss her sexual feelings with. I asked her what she wished her mother would've done back then. "I wish she'd said, 'I accept you unconditionally. I love you, and I'm sorry I don't always understand you, but I'm doing my best to accept and love you now.'" She and I did some work in the imaginal realm in which I repeated these words to her as lovingly as I could.

Of course, difference is also shaming for people who do fit the expected stereotypes. Women of all ages look into the mirror and feel terrible for not measuring up to media expectations—their breasts, or their hips, or their bellies, or thighs aren't the "right size." Men are socialized to worry about the size of their penis, and being unclothed around other boys is something to be avoided for many young men in the United States. On that topic, we'd like to share a poem one of our students wrote after hearing other men in our Sex and Shame workshop share their sexual shame:

## Finding Oneself Wanting

One's sexuality
Our sexual self and parts
At the core of our fundamental selves
Divinely bestowed via parents, borne for life
Our immutable heritable—thanks Dad!
The unfair injustice of it all

I hated my parent-given and wretched name
But a name can be changed and was
And that changed my life
I recovered my self under that alter ego
And, being released from my name shame
I felt whole again
At least, in my name

But I could not change my penis
I could not run or hide from it
Every time nature called or a comparison was made
I was reminded
Of my own painfully small, unchangeable,
Subpar, and unlovable phallus

The women I was with bore the task
Of continually reassuring a being
Already convinced of the truth
That they were being compassionately dishonest

And always looking for another
To meet their sexual needs
So, trusting a lover was an impossible setup
The pain they must have endured knowing
I would never trust them

In the gym class showers
"Stop hiding, stop being such a weakling, you sissy!"
Those words, never said, were always in my mind
Always the one guy hung to his knees
I mean, wow . . .
To me, no one could stop glans-ing at it
I went from loving gym to hating it
Terrified to reveal my tininess
And that the world would know my secret
The truth of my inadequacy
Would become a matter of public awareness
And feed my shame

My righteous shame
Of being born with something that I could never change
That made me flawed and inadequate and less than
Was going to haunt me and taunt me my whole existence
And there was nothing I could do about it
I might change my name
But there was no refrain from the eternal pain
Of bearing a tiny phallus

It took maybe twenty-five years
Of not giving up on myself
To love myself in spite of this "truth"
I could evolve and grow and heal

And see all of this differently, right?
I had to keep the faith . . . and I did
And the freedom from my shame
Was so incredibly peaceful
For once in my life
I could feel free from the shackles of my mind
It no longer controlled or possessed me
And the freedom was worth every moment of
All the painful, frustrating, humiliating, shame inducing
Work to get here

And that tiny but huge success
Makes the rest look less daunting, less scary
More possible, more loving
With more possibility for love
And I could not be more grateful

## TOUCH AND BOUNDARY VIOLATIONS

Children know when their boundaries are violated, even when they go along with whatever happens and even when they're conditioned to think it's okay. We retain this inner sense of rightness as adults, though it may be buried by years of dysfunction and social conditioning. Much of our work is helping students and clients liberate that inner wisdom and learn to pay attention to it.

A child can feel the difference between affectionate touch and sexual touch, though they may have no words for it. Sexual touch from a parent or adult relative is a severe boundary violation and causes lasting shame. That sort of violation from a person who should be safe and loving causes terrible confusion in the child; rather than being loved, soothed, and taken care of, they're being exploited for another person's gratification. The resultant scarring involves a great deal of self-attack, of feeling that one is bad or at fault. Victims of childhood sexual abuse need to learn that it wasn't their fault—that they were simply vibrant children who were taken advantage of. Inappropriate sexual touch can lead to withdrawing and rejecting connection with others. It can also lead to children believing that being sexual is the only way to get their needs met.

On the other hand, parents who hold back from showing affection to their children because they're afraid that their sexual impulses might leak out or their children may misinterpret their affections are also causing harm and confusion. Withholding is also destructive for children, who are susceptible to feeling that they are unworthy of their parents' attention—the very definition of shame.

## OUR BODIES ARE NOT ALL OF OUR SELVES

Children who don't fit the stereotypical parameters of attractiveness often grow up ashamed of their body, which can entail hiding their sexuality. Those who are told they are good-looking might do the same, or they might grow up flaunting their sexuality and attractiveness. Whatever the case, it's crucial that everyone comes to some understanding that we are far more than our sexuality or perceived attractiveness. While society might continue to be confused about this important truth, the fact that we are more than our sexuality becomes progressively clearer as we pass through adulthood.

We don't think enough about how socially determined weight and appearance are. Advertisers, the media, and social pressure distort our relationship to our body, our desire for acceptance, and our sense of a healthy, loving sexuality. The ideal weight and body size for women, for example, has changed amazingly over the past 150 years or so, and different cultures today have varying notions about what makes the female form attractive. Even so, worrying about their weight can be an endless practice of shaming for women. All of us regularly misgauge how socially engineered our expectations and desires are. Sadly, our enculturation in this matter begins when we are quite young.

### Sheila's Work with One Couple

A couple I'd been working with came into a session not long after a distressing exchange between them. The man said, "I don't know what happened. We were having pizza last night when suddenly she started screaming and ran out of the room. I had just asked her if she wanted the last piece, and then she just flipped out on me." It was clear that his retelling of the story was having a negative effect on her. She looked quite tense and distraught. When I asked her what happened, she said, "He thinks I'm fat," and the man immediately tried to convince her otherwise. Him asking her about the last piece of pizza had inadvertently kicked off her substantial body shame, which was difficult for him to understand or empathize with.

As it turns out, her family had encouraged her to watch her weight growing up, and she'd had to restrict her diet for years. It didn't take much to bring that shame immediately to the surface. Instead of him trying to convince her that she wasn't fat, I had him focus on telling her what he loved about how scrumptiously curvy her body was, which he was able to do. By the end of the session, we were able to shift the shame a little bit. Because he didn't grow up with the same kind of conditioning she had about being a woman and having her weight constantly monitored, it was easy for him to inadvertently trigger her. Both were able to learn some counter-shaming techniques, and as a result, they were better able to enjoy being sensual and sexual together.

Of course, it is not only women who have bought into the modern social stigma around weight. We have heard it over and over again from our male clients. A judgmental Attack-Other tendency can be especially hurtful as well as misleading. We often critique others because of what we don't wish to see or accept within ourselves, and the results can be particularly damaging when it comes to the sexual connection in relationships. Usually, the most helpful and effective action we can take in our relationships is to look at ourselves and see what work there is to do there.

## FULL SEXUALITY AND ECSTATIC SEX

There are many aspects to sexuality, and each can be seen as a petal on a flower. Each can be good and satisfying in itself. And each can become an end it itself, leaving out other important aspects. We see full sexuality as a many-petaled flower.

Full sexuality begins with a sense of attachment: that experience of safety and connection with another person. The security of contact and warmth is important, too, as is the pleasure of physical affection, which includes the gaze. Gaze behavior is one of the first ways that babies respond to their mothers; it's a way for them to access a tremendous amount of warmth, security, and bonding.

> It's important for everyone to know the difference between affectionate, sensual, and sexual touch.

Affectionate and sensual touch is important too—a warm hug offers all sorts of goodness. A hug can be affectionate, and it can be sensual as well. It's important for everyone to know the difference between affectionate, sensual, and sexual touch. Affectionate touch provides a sense of connection, caring, and safety. Sensual touch is designed to produce satisfaction and pleasure in itself. Sexual touch is more intense and goal directed.

Full sexuality can also involve intercourse of some kind, although it doesn't have to. Nor does full sexuality necessarily involve orgasms. We see full sexuality as involving all these elements: connection, affection, sensuality, and sexual passion.

When we experience full sexuality with a loving partner, we can enjoy a special and powerful form of love. While sex is a natural and important driving force in our lives that connects us with pleasure and our animal nature, full-loving sex offers us something even greater. Wilhelm Reich, who we mentioned earlier, believed that a person couldn't be fully sexual unless they could be fully sensual—deriving pleasure from the sensations of various parts of the body.[4] When you allow your whole body to breathe, for example, you are laying a template for sexual bliss. You can experience a sense of peace and fulfillment whenever you breathe fully, and you can feel wonderful sensual pleasure without requiring direct sex play or orgasm. To become fully sexual, you must give up control. Your body must be free enough of tension to allow intense sensations to build and flow, and your mind must be willing to surrender to those sensations.

The physical experience of orgasm is an intensified version of a full exhale. Your neck arches, your head goes back, your pelvis tilts backward so the small of your back rounds, your legs bend out with knees going toward either side, and you experience waves of sensation flowing down your body. There is also a subtle flow going up your spine as the vital energy (known in Sanskrit as *kundalini*) is activated from the spine's base. In order to experience full sexual flow, we need to be able to fully surrender to intense, all-pervasive pleasure, opening ourselves to what the French call the *little death* (their name for an orgasm). This takes trust and connection, not only within ourselves, but with the person with whom we are making love.

Reich believed that full, ecstatic sex could only take place in the context of a loving, trusting relationship, where each person, in the presence of the other, could surrender to the oceanic waves running through them. Reich also taught that the violent and destructive impulses we think of as part of human nature actually stem from our inability to experience pleasure.[5] We are born loving, he believed, and we naturally reach out to others in a loving way. Only when our loving nature is thwarted, blocked, and shamed, Reich postulated, do we turn to violence and destruction. Sexual connection can be the fullest expression of that loving, and it can reinforce our ability to love as well.

Some religions teach that celibacy is conducive to spiritual attainment. Sex, they assert, grounds us too firmly in the earthly realm, which is the realm of sin, animal behavior, desire, and disappointment. We, along with many others, believe that loving sexuality can be a path to heightened spiritual awareness. Merging with another and surrendering to the intense and transcendent feelings within us can lead to surrendering to that which is larger than ourselves—the great Oneness that includes us all.

## PRACTICE

### Sensual Pleasure

Feel free to try this exercise sitting or, if it's available to you, standing. Start by remembering something pleasant that felt especially good to you or maybe something you feel proud of: an essay you wrote, a delicious meal you enjoyed, a massage, standing in a warm patch of sunshine on a cool day. Just let yourself remember that experience and notice whatever sensations arise for you.

Pay attention to your breathing and feel into your body through your breath. Breathing in and out, allow your attention to go in with your breath through your mouth, through your throat, and into your chest. As you're doing this, see if you can locate where your good memory resides in your body. As you notice where that pleasure is, where that memory is, see if you can add a sense of warmth to it. Feel warmth expand and glow in that part of your body and notice how that sense of warmth adds to the pleasure, expands it even. Now do your best to really feel into these sensations, which are the sensations of sensual pleasure.

Finally, before concluding this practice and returning to your day, take a mental snapshot of this experience. Notice all the details you can, and see if you can preserve them to memory. After you gently bring yourself back to the room, thank yourself, and write in your journal about this experience of sensual pleasure.

10

# Returning to Relationships

*All real living is meeting. . . . When two people relate*
*to each other authentically and humanly, God is the*
*electricity that surges between them.*

—Martin Buber

Most researchers who study emotions don't think of love as one thing, but as a complex feeling state involving multiple emotions. When we talk about loving, we're referring to a reciprocal relationship. Many of us have pets, who we love and who love us back. We take care of them, and they dote on us. Cats and dogs have a big advantage over humans— they don't talk back. Unfortunately, relating to another person can be far more complex.

Although friendships and nonhuman relationships are a vital part of life, relationships with spouses or significant others, parents, children, other close relatives, and perhaps a few close friends are the most intense and also the most difficult. It's no accident that since we were quite young, our intimate relationships have been often associated with the most shame.

We've written elsewhere in the book about childhood shaming. As a reminder, our job as parents and caregivers isn't to be perfect; our job is to do our best to take care of our children and not pass our toxic shame on to them. No matter how we take care of them, in the complexity and confusion of our society, we can't always get it right. Successful parenting can be the most important job there is, but it's also the most challenging. One key with children is to accept whatever differences our children might display and modify our expectations of them according to their uniqueness and what they want out of life. To do so, it's crucial that we listen to children and receive what they tell us with compassion and sincerity.

### A Parent's Credo

As the parent of a teenager about to graduate from high school, I know I need to listen, adjust my expectations, and give advice gently. Forcing an outcome is not beneficial to anyone. Planting seeds of possibility and gently guiding allows my teen to come to her own conclusions. This allows her to trust herself and trust that I will listen and hear what she is saying.

## SHAME AND ATTACHMENT THEORY

We've mentioned John Bowlby before. Considered to be the father of Attachment Theory, Bowlby pioneered the importance of attachment in human life, especially in our early years. Our need to connect and belong starts at birth, and Bowlby's research indicates that connection is central to our survival, even as important as sleeping and eating. That driving need for connection—for a *secure base* with select others—remains with us our entire lives. Bowlby calls a sense of constancy in relationship combined with an ability to live in a full, nourishing, and free way *secure attachment*.[1] Unfortunately, children who are deprived of a secure base have trouble securely attaching to others as adults. Either we gear our actions to make sure our partner or group of friends doesn't abandon us, or we behave with the belief that we are basically alone and unsupported.

Attachment Theory focuses quite a bit on the bonds made or broken in early childhood. People first learning about Attachment Theory usually focus on how young children reach out for the care and support they need, but just as a baby's brain is wired to seek sustenance and connection, the brains of their parents and other close caregivers are also wired to give that support. Attachment Theory states that we are wired both to seek connection and to give it.

> A little bit of connection and support goes a long way, especially when it comes to lessening the burden of toxic shame.

When shame disrupts our natural tendency to support children, they suffer. When deprived of the proper nurturance and support, a child may grow up having difficulty in seeking or receiving the same as an adult. Or the now-adult child may have trouble nurturing and supporting their partner or their children. They may enter relationships still seeking what they never received as children, becoming overdemanding of the people they are closest to and thereby inadvertently reversing the usual roles in those relationships. For example, rather than receiving parental nourishment, their children are placed in a position to emotionally support their parent. This is but one way that the multigenerational transmission of shame continues.

Some of us who were deprived, neglected, or abused as children have found ways to compensate. Many of us have gone into the helping fields for that reason. While we still may have difficulty receiving care, we have learned to sustain relationships by giving. Unfortunately, we may also tend to give more than is comfortable or reasonable, leaving us feeling resentful as a result. We may also choose partners who've responded to their own childhood shame by expecting others to take care of them.

Resiliency studies have found that severely deprived children who still grew up to enjoy successful careers and relationships as adults were able to rely on at least one supportive person (a grandmother, neighbor, or teacher, for example) when they were children. In other words, a little bit of connection and support goes a long way, especially when it comes to lessening the burden of toxic shame.[2]

## TENDING AND BEFRIENDING

While psychology has stressed the amygdala responses of fight, flight, or freeze as basic to human nature, there is another system that's recently gained a prominent role in our thinking. It's called the *affiliative nervous system* by Jaak Panksepp[3] and the *ventral vagal response* by Stephen Porges,[4] whose work we discussed in chapter 7. This system sees establishing and maintaining relationships as a wired-in primal response to danger and stress, which helps humans survive.

Psychology professor Shelley Taylor, author of *The Tending Instinct* and *Social Cognition*, suggests that protecting and calming offspring may have increased survival chances for mothers and their children. Therefore, *affiliative behavior*—which promotes connection with others—is highly positive and useful. In contrast to fight, flight, or freeze, Taylor called this behavior *tend and befriend*. She also found that it coincides with the release of oxytocin, which acts as a chemical messenger in the brain that's associated with sexual arousal, recognition, trust, romantic attachment, and mother-infant bonding.[5] For this reason, oxytocin is often referred to as the *love hormone* or the *cuddle chemical*. Oxytocin production and secretion are controlled by a positive feedback mechanism in which release of the hormone stimulates even more of its own release. In other words, the more we cuddle and connect, the more we want to cuddle and connect. Oxytocin boosts feelings of love, contentment, security, and trust toward those you care about. While everyone releases oxytocin, the hormone is particularly important for women in childbirth, nursing, and child-rearing, and so women release a lot more of it.

> The things that shamed us in childhood become triggers in our relationships.

Perhaps this is correlated to the stereotype that women carry most of the burden of tending and befriending in their relationships, although men are certainly capable of doing the same. The benefits of oxytocin and the tending and befriending lifestyle are available to everyone, including men.

## INTIMACY, VULNERABILITY, AND SHAME TRIGGERS

As we said earlier, intimate relationships between partners are the most intense and most shame-prone of any adult relationships. Because they require us to once more experience the vulnerability we had in childhood, they can easily rekindle our childhood shame. We're more invested in trying to get our childhood needs met with romantic partners, so the things that shamed us in childhood become triggers in our relationships. When that occurs—as it invariably will—it's important that we understand that what's happening in the present moment is just a trigger for a shaming event that happened to us as children.

### Bret on Getting Triggered

In our culture, we have a wonderful fantasy about shame and psychological growth. We think that our issues just get better over time and they're eventually finished and resolved. I hate to break it to anyone, but even people who've worked for years on themselves, like Sheila and I, still trigger each other on a regular basis. So that means our relationship is still a work in progress. Of course, it's a lot better than it used to be between us. I'd say we have something like moderately healthy shame these days. We've reached a place in our relationship where we're able to be with each other in a healthy way most of the time, but we still experience definite ruptures that have to be healed. But when these ruptures arise, we're generally better about repairing them.

I still get upset sometimes; I still raise my voice; I still get critical. While few people have ever seen me angry, Sheila certainly has, and it can be triggering for her. Also triggering for

Sheila is when I get very precise and businesslike. "Okay, let's get this done now!" For Sheila, this interrupts her sense of flow. To Sheila, my being precise and businesslike comes across as cold and unfeeling, and she regularly ends up feeling bullied. On the other hand, I get triggered by Sheila because I often feel dropped or unimportant to her. She likes to do a lot of different things at the same time. I'll be in the middle of something with her and then the phone rings or something else catches her attention, and she immediately focuses on that. When Sheila does something like that or she's late for a time we've agreed on, it brings up my feelings of abandonment and triggers memories of being ignored by my parents, who were locked in their own shame loop. I may have to take a timeout and do some breathing or walk around the block to calm myself down.

Different things set us off. Verbal shaming, feeling ignored, physical and emotional abuse . . . all of these are common triggers. But shame triggers aren't always as obvious. Some people react strongly to feeling lectured, to feeling like they're a disappointment to their partner, or to being "the bad guy" in the relationship. Other people have a really hard time being turned down or being told no by their partner, especially when it comes to sex. For others, it's triggering to be told to calm down because we can feel like we're being told to stuff our feelings, just as we were shamed into doing as children.

## GENDER AND INTIMATE RELATIONSHIPS

There are many differences between partners that must be negotiated, and shame comes out of difference. How do we communicate our needs when the other person seems so different from us? Various challenges can also arise when the race, age, class, and gender of partners are different. This topic is way too large for this book to cover, as is the topic of gender in today's world. In this section, we're going to use the terms *men* and *women* to reference those who have been socialized as "men" and "women."

We hope you'll take these generalizations for what they are, recognizing that all generalizations are limited, and find some usefulness in them, no matter who you're attracted to or how you identify.

As we noted above, women tend to be more inclined toward tending and befriending, and men are usually more susceptible to fight-or-flight dynamics in relationships. Of course, much of this is socialization, as boys and girls are treated differently from the moment they are born. Linguistics professor Deborah Tannen, author of *You Just Don't Understand*, points to experiments that show that as young as seven, boys tend to feel they have to solve problems by themselves and support each other by saying, in some form, "We don't have to talk about your problem. I know you can handle it." On the other hand, girls seek out emotional support and offer the same to other girls.[6]

In couples, men often feel responsible for keeping everyone happy, and they approach problems as immediately fixable things, thereby offering quick-fix solutions. If his wife comes home angry about her boss, a husband may immediately suggest, "You don't have to take that. Why don't you quit?" Women, on the other hand, are more likely to want to process their feelings and talk problems out. John Gottman, who's written a number of books on working with couples, has found that when there's a breach or argument in the relationship, men's heart rates and other vital signs go through the roof, whereas women's fluctuate only a little.[7] Further, John Gray, author of *Men Are from Mars, Women Are from Venus*, suggests that *when there's a problem, men go into their cave to be alone, while women go to the well to be with other women.*[8]

## PURSUERS AND WITHDRAWERS

There's another way to discuss this dynamic—one that doesn't require gender specificity. Regardless of our gender or identity, we humans have two basic yet conflicting needs: autonomy (independence) and belonging (connection). Even though we all have both needs, most of us are more aware of—or more strongly pulled toward—one or the other.

The way this usually plays out in relationships is that we tend to be drawn to people who favor the other need. If we're more concerned with independence, we're usually drawn to someone who's more interested in the connection side of things. And if we value belonging more, we tend to get involved with people who are invested in their own autonomy. This can feel like a cruel joke at times, but it's actually an interesting way that both needs are represented in any given relationship.

Sue Johnson is a pioneer in this work. In her terms, the partner who strives most for connection is the *pursuer*, and one who's more after independence is the *withdrawer*.[9] Pursuers and withdrawers tend to find and marry each other (like us—Bret is the pursuer, and Sheila is the withdrawer). Although we are attracted to people of the opposite tendency, the difference can be hard to handle, and both people can easily find their childhood shame getting triggered. More often than not, pursuers had childhoods marked with feelings of abandonment, and withdrawers experienced more invasion of their boundaries. Pursuers are more likely to feel alone, so they exert more energy trying to avoid that feeling by constantly reaching out and seeking connection. Withdrawers, on the other hand, are likely to feel invaded, bullied, or dominated; therefore, they tend to pull inward, shut down, and keep quiet to avoid whatever contact they perceive as threatening. Pursuers tend to be extroverted, and withdrawers introverted. The pursuer does the reaching out, sets up activities to do as a couple, makes plans, and initiates conversations. The withdrawer tends to want to be alone more, partake in solo activities (or with friends without the partner), needs more privacy, and takes more time to think before speaking.

Both types need connection and independence, but the amount they need differs. If the pursuer gets burned-out and stops pursuing, the distance may become too great for the withdrawer, which prompts them to reach out. Psychologist George Bach suggests that all couples' fights are actually about distance—one person wants to be closer than the other does. This holds true for both pursuers and withdrawers.[10]

In any relationship, it's vital to understand whether you're the pursuer or the withdrawer. One common issue for pursuers arises when the withdrawer fails to follow through with an agreement or they do so in a way the pursuer doesn't approve of. Accordingly, pursuers focus on what didn't go as planned, which usually involves some degree of complaint, criticism, and blame (Sue Johnson calls the pursuer the *pursuer-blamer*). Unfortunately, informing our partner of what they didn't do right is known to trigger shame, which can freeze them and make it even more unlikely that we'll get what we want. For this reason, it's helpful for pursuers to speak in terms of what they want and need, as opposed to focusing on what feels lacking. *I* language is useful in this regard: "I had an expectation that . . ." instead of "You were supposed to . . ." for example.

Withdrawers are often oblivious to the problems as pursuers see them. The problem for withdrawers tends to be the pursuer's blame. They're overwhelmed with their subsequent feelings of shame, of being invaded again, and so they try to placate the angry pursuer to make the criticism stop. Either that or they withdraw into silence or, in some cases, leave the relationship entirely.

## A Withdrawer's Reflection on Attachment Trauma

I feel like my last intimate relationship was the definition of toxic shame. Of course, there was attachment trauma. What I am visualizing in this moment is the endless arguments over groceries, constantly avoiding communication, not being seen, heard, understood, et cetera. As I peel back the layers, it seems shame was driving the bus. Which then evoked a sense of powerlessness in my life. I felt alone in this relationship, even with her sitting beside me. I found other ways to help me not feel this way, which was through harmful behaviors, such as drugs, alcohol, other women, sex, and anything else I could get my hands on.

Pursuers tend to feel as if they're doing everything they can to sustain their relationship. That leaves them feeling the same loneliness they experienced as children. Although pursuers are known to engage in Attack-Other reactions ("There's something wrong with *you*"), beneath that, their shame voice is suggesting quite the opposite (*There's something wrong with me. No one can give me what I need. I just need too much. That's why I can't get my needs met.*). That Attack-Self tendency is more overt for withdrawers: *I'll never be enough for them* and *I blew it again* are common messages. When there's a conflict, both sides act to resolve it the best they know how: the pursuer wants to resolve things quickly and get everything back to normal, and the withdrawer wants to keep quiet, let things pass, and not make matters worse. Unfortunately, these different approaches often escalate the conflict, as the pursuer surges forward for connection, and the withdrawer backpedals to gain space and ground. Each is expressing a need their partner can't handle in the moment.

While this is a common scenario, it doesn't have to continue. The impasse can be broken, the conflict softened. Understanding these common relational differences can help the pursuer give the withdrawer their needed space and encourage the withdrawer to reassure their partner by speaking up and describing what's going on for them (for example, "I'm too agitated to discuss this right now. I'll be back in a little while, and we can talk then."). Pursuers and withdrawers usually suffered different types of difficulty in childhood, and they therefore march to completely different relational drummers. That means conflicts will invariably arise. However, with proper tools, compassion, and goodwill, conflicts can be minimized and eventually repaired. While there are times when one or the other will behave so outrageously that most of the upset is really happening in the present moment, in most cases, recognizing the 90/10 Split can help both calm down and ultimately resolve the conflict and reestablish a loving connection.

### Sheila's Pursuing and Withdrawing Clients

One couple I worked with even had difficulty sitting together in the session. That's how rough it had become. They no longer felt much connection between them, and they decided to give therapy one more try before getting a divorce. Both wanted the relationship, but it was extremely uncomfortable for them.

Being the pursuer in this couple, he told her, "I can count on one hand the times you've reached out to me since we've been together." When I checked in with her to see how that landed, she said, "That's it. I never get it right." She was always feeling put down by him and insufficient. After a while, the two were at least able to express curiosity about the other's needs. "Why do you tell Sheila all this stuff while we're in session, but when we're at home you don't talk to me the same way?" he asked. The woman replied, "Sheila asks how I'm doing and then gives me a lot of space to answer. It helps me figure it out and connect with what's going on." He realized that he'd been pursuing her so passionately that she was withdrawing, and that realization helped slow the cycle some. In turn, that decreased the ruptures between them, his criticism of her, and her actions that made him feel even more abandoned. Over time, they were able to accept my invitation to remember how they were drawn to each other in the first place, partake in some intimacy exercises, and appreciate the connection they still shared.

Ruptures in attachment encourage negative cycles between couples, but sometimes it just takes a little compassion and understanding to turn the trajectory of the relationship in the other direction. Instead of more alienation, pain, and shame, couples can meaningfully connect with kindness that recently felt alien to them. It's a lot easier to rebuild the bridge when shame isn't running the show.

## LET'S TALK ABOUT SEX

Pursuer and withdrawer dynamics are challenging enough to deal with, but everything in a relationship becomes more charged when a couple's sexual connection is in question. For many couples, their sex life is the epitome of their connection. Sex between loving partners can be the best experience imaginable, but it's also the place most susceptible to shame and shame triggers.

### A Student Wonders: What's Wrong with Me in Bed?

For the last several months, I have experienced what I thought was sexual rejection (I made it all about me when my fiancé did not want to engage in physical intimacy), as I did not know the root cause. Unbeknownst to me, my fiancé has been dealing with low testosterone as well as low libido and was afraid to share that with me. As a result, he made excuses as to why physical intimacy was not possible (headache, backache, gastrointestinal problems, work stress, et cetera).

When I shared with him my enthusiasm about the shame work I'd been doing, he opened up to me and divulged the truth about what was going on. He said he'd been afraid to tell me and that it broke his heart that I thought he was no longer attracted to me. He also said that he knew that he needed to confide in me and that he was wrong for not having done so earlier; he said that he was scared that I would leave him due to his current physical issue. My fiancé had been living with so much shame about his issue, and as a result, he withdrew from me, which changed our dynamic in ways that didn't feel good to either of us.

His withdrawal and my perception of it as a rejection triggered my shame. I blamed myself (for being overweight, not attractive enough, et cetera) and he blamed himself (he needed to lose weight, didn't exercise enough, didn't manage his work stress well). As a result of feeling rejected, I was critical at times and not as loving to him. He's extremely sensitive to feeling that he's not doing things correctly, so my criticism spurred even more of his shame. He'd respond to that with a louder, sterner voice, which, in turn, triggered me even more! And that's how our shame dance went for far too long until he opened up and we both came clean.

We're working together on it now. Although it's difficult not being as physically intimate as we were before, we're hopeful that the issue will eventually get remedied. There's still shame, but we're more open and honest with our feelings than we have ever been. The disconnection that occurred before created a lot of rupture, and we're still healing from that while finding other ways to be intimate. I'm choosing to look at this situation as a huge opportunity for us to have a closer and more spiritually connected relationship.

## CONNECTING WITH LANGUAGE STYLES

There have been a number of books devoted to language styles published over the years (including Gary Chapman's brilliant *The Five Love Languages*) that couples have picked up to regain connection and facilitate repair. We like to employ a theory of effective communication (developed by Bret) that conceives of four different language styles we can use to express ourselves and understand others better. Those styles are *love*, *power*, *facts*, and *vision*. These four styles can be thought of as two pairs of opposites: love language is radically different from power language, for example, and vision language differs substantially from the language of facts. Although people tend to favor only one or two of those languages, it's extremely helpful to learn how to access the others, especially when it comes to relationships.

Love language is affiliative. It's designed to establish and maintain connection. Common phrases in this language include "I love you" (obviously), "I miss you," "You matter to me," "I care," "Thank you," and "I'm sorry." This style uses the word *I* a lot and is fairly adept at expressing feelings.

The power language style has two branches: self-empowerment and power over others. The difference between these is quite stark. The first is more assertive and—like the love style—tends toward *I* statements ("I want," "I feel," "I need," and "I deserve"). The more aggressive power style, however, employs a lot of *you* language: "What's wrong with you?" "You better do what I say," and "You're the problem here." Aggressive power is known for its shaming statements and for how it situates the speaker as superior. This style comes from seeing the world as hierarchical—either you win or I do. While there's certainly a place for this language at times (and we all need to know how to deal with it when someone's using it), it can prove quite harmful to relationships.

Factual language (as in *Dragnet*'s "Just the facts, ma'am") is precise and quite useful, but somewhat limited. Additionally, as we've seen recently in the United States, employing what we call *false factual* has become a popular approach to serve oneself. A more personal version of the false factual is when we label major events or feelings as *no big deal*, when clearly they are. Power statements can mask themselves with false factual language too ("There's only one way to do this" and "I really didn't have a choice" are common examples).

Finally, the vision-language style employs the *we* pronoun a lot, and it addresses a shared future, often in a motivating way ("We shall overcome," for example). We rely on vision language when we need to motivate ourselves and inspire others.

Knowledge of these languages and the ability to use them appropriately can help us get more of what we want from other people and create more successful relationships of every kind. In the same way, it's helpful to check what kind of language that you and others are using. Generally, we need a balance of all the language styles, and this balance varies across different situations. With intimate partners, love language is most crucial, with just the right touch of factual, assertive power, and vision language. If you're involved in an argument or disagreement and don't want it to escalate any further, it's a good idea to avoid power language and emphasize the other three. At work, factual language is typically primary, although assertive power is essential when interviewing for a job or asking for a raise. Using vision language by describing what you want to see happening for the company and how you can help that come about would also be important. In all cases, it's ideal to gear our language carefully to the person we're speaking with, and nowhere is this truer than in intimate relationships.

## LANGUAGE STYLES

See if you can feel into which one of the four language styles you prefer. Which is your second choice? Which is most difficult for you? Write them down if you like. Now, think of someone whom you're in close relationship with and see if you can get a sense of which language style they prefer. There's a good chance it won't be your first preference. If it is, congratulations. You can choose someone else you care about or cared about in the past. If your language preferences differ, think about how you could use their preferred language more of the time. See if you can think of a specific topic that has been difficult to discuss in the past and write down what words you could use now to address it, words that are in their language preference. Note any resistance that comes up. Imagine trying this style in a real conversation.

In the book *Difficult Conversations*, the authors suggest that there are always three conversations going on at the same time: the *what happened* conversation, the *feelings* conversation, and the *identity* conversation.[11] We're usually most aware of the first, but the other two are just as important. Conversations bring up feelings, and we need to acknowledge and talk about the feelings involved. While some of us do share our feelings when we talk, the third conversation—which may be the most important—is often kept secret, even from ourselves. While we're talking away about what happened and how we feel about it, we're also thinking about what the conversation says about what kind of person we are. In our terms, this is the shame conversation.

Remember that shame thrives on secrecy. If we never attend to this third conversation, shame continues to grow, and we make it more difficult to learn about ourselves and share that. We also fail to recognize that the very same internal conversation is happening for others. When we become more sensitive to shame in ourselves and others, we can take it into account when speaking and listening. It becomes much more possible to connect in an effective and loving way. Compassion for unconscious shame reactions in ourselves and others can start to change the dynamics of all our relationships.

> Shame is not just a feeling; it's a major factor in determining who we are.

## HEALTHY RELATIONSHIPS

In most cases, the relationships we have with our parents, children, and intimate partners are the most intense and important of all. Of course, we'll have other significant relationships during our lives, each with varying levels of connection, which means that our shame can become triggered in all sorts of ways with a wide assortment of people. For this reason, it's vital to understand when your childhood shame has been triggered and respond appropriately in the present moment. In many cases, that could mean realizing when you're withdrawing and speaking up or realizing you're pursuing and blaming and trying something different. It's also crucial to know which relationships are worth keeping. To paraphrase the song famously sung by Kenny Rogers, you've got to know when it's time to hold and when it's time to fold. Sometimes, the desire to repair is one-sided, or it's clear that what's on the other side of the bridge isn't someplace you wish to go. Whether the relationship is worth the work or whether it's time to cut your losses and move on is ultimately up to you.

It's vital that we pay attention to our internal conversations and learn from them. It's equally important that we realize that the same conversations go on in other people. If we are sensitive to shame in ourselves and others, we can take that into account. Shame is not just a feeling; it's a major factor in determining who we are. As we become more aware of the shame conversation and determine how much the shame is coming from the present or from the past, we will come to enjoy healthier, more successful relationships.

# Conclusion

We want to celebrate you and thank you for journeying through this book with us. Helping people transform shame has been our goal and passion for many years, and we hope you have benefited and that you'll help us spread the word. Although we are ending the book here, the journey goes on—both for you and for us. It's our hope that you now feel empowered to create a healthy relationship with shame—to understand it better, lessen its harmful effects, and embrace it as a tool for growth.

This book is one more step on our journey of lifting the veil of mystery and revulsion that coats shame and makes it so difficult to deal with. We believe that unacknowledged shame leads to much of the conflict and violence in the world, both personal and political. We are proud and grateful to have been able to train so many therapists, coaches, and other helping professionals to help others transform their shame. This book is our next step. It is our attempt to directly reach people on the individual and global levels because we're convinced that addressing shame directly and working to transform it will decrease hatred and misunderstanding and help the world be more compassionate and just.

The idea of the evolutionary purpose of shame is different for all of us. For Sheila, it was part of a lifetime of inner work to heal her shyness and become more assertive. For Bret, it was a multiyear journey to develop gentleness and let go of arrogance and perfectionism. For both of us, it led to creating more ways to assist people in exploring their shame, sharing with others, and finding new energy and purpose.

Please continue to use all the tools you've acquired in this book—not just the practices and reflections, but also a new approach to self-compassion in which your kind inner coach is a more compelling voice than your inner critic. We also hope you'll regularly check in on your inner child. How's that young part of you doing? What do they need? What are their hopes and fears?

We hope this book has touched you and opened some doors for you to grow and change. Despite your best efforts, shame will find a way to sneak up on you when you least expect it, and no doubt you will occasionally find yourself upset and frozen again, just as we do. However, you can now better understand it as it happens, realize that you're in the grip of shame, and learn from the process rather than simply reacting, denying, or becoming overwhelmed. You can now view shame as a normal human emotion, accept whatever it has to teach you, and let the rest go. In the words of Martin Luther King Jr., "We must accept finite disappointment, but never lose infinite hope."

# Note for Therapists, Coaches, and Other Helping Professionals

If you are reading this section after working through the concepts and exercises in this book, congratulations. When you have worked on your own shame, and with the foundation offered in this book, you can better help clients deal with their shame without trying to avoid it or being triggered by it. Talking about shame can be difficult and confusing. It can also be a welcome presence in an incredibly difficult world. Many clients are caught up in Attack-Other or Deny reactions to their shame and may not even be aware that they have shame. Others are in an Attack-Self reaction and awash with shame or in a Withdraw reaction and reluctant to engage. Knowing that shame can underly all these reactions can be helpful.

We teach our students, who are all helping professionals, to blend the qualities of trusted expert and caring friend, to be curious and engage the client's curiosity, as well as to be kind and compassionate. In our work, we educate about what shame is and how it affects our nervous system. We normalize shame as a primary emotion that everyone shares. And, since shame is an under-resourced state, we help clients find and expand their resources, both internal and external. We also reveal a little bit about ourselves to help level the playing field, as shame makes people feel one-down. We find commonalities with clients and acknowledge differences as well. We acknowledge that we have limitations, that we are also limited human beings. We may be experts on shame, but they are experts on themselves. As shame exists in the body as well as in the mind, we make sure that we are breathing and feeling grounded and then encourage our clients to breathe and feel physically present as well.

We encourage you to utilize all the resources on our website (healingshame.com). We have many free videos and articles that may help you learn more about shame. We also offer many online workshops that deal with different aspects of shame, which can lead to certification as a Healing Shame Practitioner, as well as private consultations.

We hope that this book has brought new insight and a growing sense of being able to help clients get more comfortable with this mysterious and powerful emotion. We look forward to meeting you again in a more interactive way.

# Resources

We are very committed to provide all the resources we possibly can to help you understand, reduce, and transform toxic shame. We have gathered many of these on our website: healingshame.com. There, you'll find a number of articles, webinars, and videos—all free.

We also offer an extensive reading list on the website of books we consider to be most basic to healing shame, both for individuals and for professional helpers. Additionally, our Sounds True audio series on Healing Shame is available through the publisher, our website, Amazon, Audible, and Barnes and Noble.

We have over fifteen different training workshops available to therapists, coaches, teachers, nurses, healers, religious leaders, and other helping professionals, as well as a complete training program leading to certification as a Healing Shame Practitioner in the Lyon/Rubin Method.

There is also a list of Healing Shame Practitioners on our website, that includes practitioners from all over the world, with their photos and short biographies. As we suggest, the journey to healing shame can be much smoother with the help and guidance of a helping professional. There are many competent and caring helping professionals out there whom we have not trained. If you are working with or reaching out to a helping professional, we suggest that you ask them how they work with shame and see if it makes sense to you. We also suggest that, if it feels appropriate, you recommend this book.

Sheila also teaches a separate program called Embodied Life Stories that can be found on her website: sheilarubin.com.

# Acknowledgments

We'd like to thank our wonderful Healing Shame students and Practitioners, without whom this book would not have been possible. It truly took a community.

We want to thank first our amazing coordinator, Elizabeth Davidge, who is now a Healing Shame Practitioner, and who has done so much, both for our workshops and for creating the book, and Kristi Coombs, tech savant, who brought us into the computer age.

We want to especially thank our students, who have contributed directly to the book with stories or moral support. All are helping professionals, and most are certified, or will soon be certified, as Healing Shame Practitioners. They are: Jeff LaMie, who has contributed enormously to Bret's well-being and his ability to write this book; Stephanie Holmes-Farmer, who helped us a great deal in our process; Adele Zinberg, cousin, friend, and constant inspiration; Jennifer Kindera; Christie Batt; Beverly de Witt-Moylan; Lauren Gray; Harald Bettger; Dustin Dutcher; Brian Uhlin; Jen Meller; Stephanie Lee; Dolores D'Amato; A. J. Bond; Jill Anderson; Pernille Melsted; and Erin Martin.

Other students and practitioners, not as directly involved in the book, but equally important to us and to the work: Gail Van Buuren, Elaine Sohier-Gayler, Barbara McCoard, Joan Gold, Fran Schwartz, Phebe Fletcher, Kimberly Chan, Cori Soliz, Tatra de la Rosa, Freddie Barahona, Joy Metoyer, Amy Doublet, Sarah Liebman, Stu Neft, Marion Klein, and many, many others. Also Brian Mahan, who holds a special place in our history and the development of our work.

Inspirational friends and colleagues include John Amodeo; Bruce Ecker; Ann Weiser Cornell; Igor Weiss; Joel and Anne Isaacs; Rulik Perla; Soonja Kim; Andrea Flanders; Chris Volker; long-time photographer Lea Delson; and Tracy Jones, who was like a midwife to Sheila in birthing the book proposal and who designed both of our incredible websites. Bret also wants to thank Mark Waldman and Austin Anton, colleagues from the old days.

We want to thank Diana Fosha, Sue Johnson, and Peter Levine for their amazing trainings. Bret specially wants to thank Al Bauman, who opened his eyes to the work of Wilhelm Reich and the wisdom of the body. Also, through their writings: Gershen Kaufman, Donald Nathanson, Silvan Tomkins, Terrence Real, John Bradshaw, Rachel Naomi Remen, and Brené Brown, among many others.

Finally, we want to thank our amazing editor, Robert Lee, a willing and wonderful collaborator, who was able to cut our manuscript by 50 percent and actually make it better. We want to thank all the people at Sounds True, especially Tami Simon and Anastasia Pellouchoud, for believing in our work and nurturing us through the difficult writing process. Also, Mitchell Clute and Aron Arnold for their hands-on help in producing and engineering our *Healing Shame* audio series.

More from Sheila: Renée Emunah, director of CIIS Drama Therapy department, for creating the Drama Therapy program and especially "self-revelatory performance." For Adam Blatner, who kept writing to me so many times years ago. I couldn't believe that he really wanted my chapter in his book. That started my clinical writing. For Corey Fisher and Helen Stolfitz of A Traveling Jewish Theater Company for the format of the life story process; Sally Bailey for inspiration; Marja and Tracy and Regina for helping me vision so much of this and more. For my Embodied Life Story students and anyone who's Self-Rev performance I directed. For Evelie Posch for singing and for all the storytellers and story weavers and authors who came before with something a little different. And Marcia Kimmel of The Next Stage; Laurie, Laura, Kay, and Patricia in Portland; and Linda Soloy, who was my first witness. Also Mark Alter, I have you all in my heart.

And for anyone else we haven't mentioned, we sincerely apologize. We couldn't possibly name you all.

# Notes

## Chapter 1: Shame—The Magic Emotion

1. Brené Brown, "Shame vs. Guilt," January 15, 2013, brenebrown
.com/articles/2013/01/15/shame-v-guilt/.

2. Gershen Kaufman, "The Meaning of Shame: Toward a Self-Affirming Identity," *Journal of Counseling Psychology* 21, no. 6 (1974): 568-574.

## Chapter 2: Unlocking Shame Binds

1. Bruce K. Alexander, "Addiction: The View from the Rat Park (2010)," brucekalexander.com/articles-speeches/rat-park/148 -addiction-the-view-from-rat-park.

2. South African History Online, "M. K. Gandhi Is Forcibly Removed from a Whites-Only Train Carriage," sahistory.org.za/dated-event /mk-gandhi-forcibly-removed-whites-only-train-carriage; South African History Online, "44. Gandhi Explains 'Satyagraha,'" sahistory .org.za/archive/44-gandhi-explains-satyagraha.

3. Adam J. Frank and Elizabeth A. Wilson, *A Silvan Tompkins Handbook: Foundations for Affect Theory* (Minneapolis: University of Minnesota Press, 2020).

## Chapter 3: Reactions to Shame

1. Donald Nathanson, *Shame and Pride: Affect, Sex, and the Birth of the Self* (New York: W. W. Norton & Company, 1994).

2. John Bradshaw, *Healing the Shame That Binds You* (Deerfield Beach, FL: Health Communications, 2005).

3. Pete Walker, "Codependency, Trauma, and the Fawn Response," January–February 2003, pete-walker.com /codependencyFawnResponse.htm.

## Chapter 4: Healthy Shame

1. John Amodeo, "Can Shame Be Your Friend?" *Psychology Today*, June 10, 2016, psychologytoday.com/us/blog/intimacy-path -toward-spirituality/201606/can-shame-be-your-friend.

2. Eugene Gendlin, *Focusing* (New York: Bantam Dell, 2007).

3. Michelle Obama, *Becoming* (New York: Crown Publishing Group, 2018).

4. Brené Brown, "The Power of Vulnerability," December 23, 2010, TED, ted.com/talks/brene_brown_the_power_of_vulnerability ?language=en.

5. Albert Einstein, *Living Philosophies* (New York: Simon & Schuster, 1931).

## Chapter 5: Shame and Your Inner Child

1. Edward Tronick et al., "The Infant's Response to Entrapment Between Contradictory Messages in Face-to-Face Interaction," *Journal of the American Academy of Child and Adolescent Psychiatry* 17 (Winter 1978): 1–13.

2. Linda Alsop-Shields and Heather Mohay, "John Bowlby and James Roberson: Theorists, Scientists, and Crusaders for Improvements in the Care of Children in Hospital," *Journal of Advanced Nursing* 35, no. 1 (December 20, 2001).

3. Donald Winnicott, *Playing and Reality* (New York: Routledge, 2005).

## Chapter 6: Healing Your Inner Child

1. Renée Emunah, *Acting for Real: Drama Therapy Process, Technique, and Performance* (New York: Routledge, 1994), 33.

2. Robert Landy, *Drama Therapy: Concepts, Theories, and Practices* (Springfield, IL: Charles C. Thomas Books, 1994).

## Chapter 7: Shame and Trauma

1. International Association of Trauma Recovery Coaching, Internal training manual.

2. Stephen W. Porges, *The Pocket Guide to the Polyvagal Theory: The Transformative Power of Feeling Safe* (New York: W. W. Norton & Company, 2017).

3. Wilhelm Reich, *Character Analysis*, trans. Vincent Carfagno (New York: Farrar, Straus, and Giroux, 1972).

4. Barbara Ferry, ed., *The Amygdala: A Discrete Multitasking Manager* (Rijeka, Croatia: InTech, 2014).

5. Bessel van der Kolk, *The Body Keeps the Score: Brain, Mind, and Body in the Healing of Trauma* (New York: Penguin, 2014).

6. Gus Van Sant, dir., *Good Will Hunting* (Los Angeles: Miramax Films, 1997).

7. Daniel J. Siegel, *The Developing Mind: How Relationships and the Brain Interact to Shape Who We Are* (New York: Guilford Press, 2020).

## Chapter 8: Shame and the Body

1. Anita A. Johnston, *Eating in the Light of the Moon: How Women Can Transform Their Relationship with Food Through Myths, Metaphors, and Storytelling* (Carlsbad, CA: Gurze Books, 1996).

## Chapter 9: Sex, Pleasure, and Shame

1. Wilhelm Reich, *The Function of the Orgasm: Sex-Economic Problems of Biological Energy*, trans. Vincent Carfagno (New York: Farrar, Straus, and Giroux, 1973).

2. Wilhelm Reich, *The Mass Psychology of Fascism*, trans. Vincent Carfagno (New York: Farrar, Straus, and Giroux, 1970).

3. Reich, *The Function of the Orgasm.*

4. Reich, *The Function of the Orgasm.*

5. Reich, *The Function of the Orgasm.*

## Chapter 10: Returning to Relationships

1. John Bowlby, *A Secure Base: Parent-Child Attachment and Healthy Human Development* (New York: Basic Books, 1988).

2. Ann S. Masten, Karin M. Best, and Norman Garmezy, "Resilience and Development: Contributions from the Study of Children Who Overcome Adversity," *Development and Psychopathology* 4, no. 2 (October 1990): 425–444, doi.org/10 .1017/S0954579400005812.

3. Jaak Panksepp, *Affective Neuroscience: The Foundations of Human and Animal Emotions* (Oxford: Oxford University Press, 1998).

4. Porges, *The Pocket Guide to the Polyvagal Theory.*

5. Shelley E. Taylor, "Tend and Befriend Theory," in *Handbook of Theories of Social Psychology*, eds. Paul A. M. Van Lange, Arie W. Kruglanski, and E. Tory Higgins (Los Angeles, CA: Sage Publications, 2012).

6. Deborah Tannen, *You Just Don't Understand: Women and Men in Conversation* (New York: HarperCollins, 2001).

7. John Gottman, *Why Marriages Succeed or Fail: And How You Can Make Yours Last* (New York: Simon & Schuster, 1994).

8. John Gray, *Men Are from Mars, Women Are from Venus: The Classic Guide to Understanding the Opposite Sex* (New York: HarperCollins, 2004).

9. Sue Johnson, *Hold Me Tight: Seven Conversations for a Lifetime of Love* (New York: Little, Brown, and Company, 2008).

10. George Bach and Peter Wyden, *The Intimate Enemy: How to Fight Fair in Love and Marriage* (New York: Avon, 1983).

11. Douglas Stone, Bruce Patton, and Sheila Heen, *Difficult Conversations: How to Discuss What Matters Most* (New York: Penguin, 2010).

# About the Authors

Bret Lyon, PhD, SEP, and Sheila Rubin, MA, LMFT, RDT/BCT, are long-time helping professionals who have devoted the last twenty years of their lives to healing shame. They are the founders and co-directors of the Center for Healing Shame. Through their popular workshops, they have taught thousands of therapists, coaches, and other helping professionals from all over the world how to more effectively identify and work with shame.

Sheila is a licensed marriage and family therapist, a registered drama therapist, and has taught at JFK University and CIIS, as well as being the eating disorder specialist at a hospital and directing Embodied Life Stories performances. Bret holds doctorates in both psychology and drama and has taught at Tufts University, Pomona College, and the American Academy of Dramatic Arts, as well as written and directed plays in regional theater and off-off Broadway.

Sheila and Bret are married and live in a wooded, hilly area of Oakland, California, with their two cats, Logan Tigger III and Sedona Sonoma, the Magic Cat. When they are not working to heal the planet through healing shame, Sheila devotes herself to painting, and Bret puts his soul into photographing birds and other wildlife. Please visit healingshame.com to discover more about them and their work.

# About Sounds True

Sounds True was founded in 1985 by Tami Simon with a clear mission: to disseminate spiritual wisdom. Since starting out as a project with one woman and her tape recorder, we have grown into a multimedia publishing company with a catalog of more than 3,000 titles by some of the leading teachers and visionaries of our time, and an ever-expanding family of beloved customers from across the world.

In more than three decades of evolution, Sounds True has maintained our focus on our overriding purpose and mission: to wake up the world. We offer books, audio programs, online learning experiences, and in-person events to support your personal growth and awakening, and to unlock our greatest human capacities to love and serve.

At SoundsTrue.com you'll find a wealth of resources to enrich your journey, including our weekly *Insights at the Edge* podcast, free downloads, and information about our nonprofit Sounds True Foundation, where we strive to remove financial barriers to the materials we publish through scholarships and donations worldwide.

To learn more, please visit SoundsTrue.com/freegifts or call us toll-free at 800.333.9185.

Together, we can wake up the world.

**sounds true**
WAKING UP THE WORLD